Irish Gandy Dancer

A tale of building the Transcontinental Railroad

by

Dr. Ryan Michael Collins

Table of Contents

Photographs located in the middle of the book

Dedication: To my daughters Rebecca and Sarah. May you and your children appreciate this collection of tales the same way I did with my father.

Author's Note

There are almost no published journals, diaries or correspondence of workers that built the Transcontinental Railroad following the closure of the Civil War. This is somewhat a paradox considering so many records exist on both sides, North and South, that give us a grass roots view of the conflict that had ripped the country apart just a few months before.

The Union victory in the Civil War had the effect of cementing the relationship between the Northern and Southern states, albeit it was at best an uneasy and conflicted partnership. In a similar fashion, the construction of the Transcontinental Railroad had a similar profound effect of permanently tying the Eastern and Western United States together, clearing the way for expansion of the country that had recently reaffirmed its status as an indivisible nation.

Most of the historic accounts of the construction of the transcontinental railroad take a top down view of the events, places and people that influenced the story. The story that follows approaches the tale differently, taking a bottom up approach of the events and attempting to explain them through the perspective of a young Irish laborer. The reasons for this approach are that it will hopefully offer a different point of view than the traditional broad based view so pervasive in historic accounts. Secondly, history is always viewed through one set of eyes and the historian by nature compiles data and makes an estimate of what everyone saw. The result is often diluted and diminishes the personal effect events have on the players. Third, many historic accounts are top heavy with dates, facts and places, forgetting that the people who make history are flesh and blood human beings with flaws and heroic abilities, all rolled into the same package. They experience feelings of elation and boredom, fear and anger, apathy and pride. I believe it is critical to flavor the tale with these emotions because emotions, not the intellect are what drive us to be the people we are.

One other noteworthy aspect of this story is the style of the narrative. Many contextual references found here are balancing acts between the Victorian language prevalent for the day and that easily understood by readers in the 21st century. This means the colloquial speech used by 19th century Irish laborers, reflecting their world view and prejudices were employed whenever it had the desired effect while at the same time striving for clarity for the modern day reader.

The aim of this book, quite frankly, is to build a bridge between readers of the 21st century with the young, poor and adventurous people of the post Civil War era who literally had nothing but their names and strong backs to sustain them. It is unquestionably a daunting task because the conditions these young laborers endured to make a better life for themselves seem Herculean by modern day standards. Still, it is these people who went before that set the standard for those that followed, all the while building a nation and doing so with no individual memories of record for those who sacrificed so much. As one of the heirs who has benefited from their sacrifice, I would like to thank those who took up the shovel, pick and maul to make a better future for their children, grandchildren and all others who came behind.

Personal effect of John Joseph McGlinchey

December 1865

This is the written account of John Joseph McGlinchey, born March 13, 1846 in Donegal, County Donegal Ireland, migrated to Philadelphia, Pennsylvania at age of 3. It is my very own hand that is recording this account of my life that I shall begin during the recent troubles. I was a drover during the War Between the States, bringing cattle to the Union Army, riding drag at the age of 15, mainly for the 116th Pennsylvania Regiment that was fighting throughout the South. After the war, many a man including myself could not find employment earning wages beyond those that kept a man out of the poor house and certainly nothing to support a wife and children. My fellow countrymen continue to pour into the cities such as Philadelphia, New York and Boston off the coffin ships, looking for work and willing to do it for half the wage a man should. I managed to hold on to my wages that I earned during the war but have nearly exhausted what remains. Soon, I was thinking to myself, I shall be like my newly arrived countrymen with the clothes on my back and nothing in my stomach.

Providence reached out to me one day and I was recruited as part of a work gang digging grades and filling cuts for the tracks from Omaha, Nebraska Territory for the Union Pacific Railroad. The work promises to be hard and dangerous as the Indians in the territories often attack those that venture into their hunting ground with ferocity and efficiency. All of Philadelphia is astir with the thought of joining the country together in a grand project such as this. Those who are organizing this scheme are looking for strong backs to dig at upwards of two dollars per day with meals and a place to sleep off the ground. Compared to my recent employment of riding drag while droving cattle, the possibility of being struck dead by a Tennessee sharpshooter or slowly starving in the familiar surroundings of Philadelphia, I fear there was little difference if I should stay put and face certain doom or cast my lot with this adventure and head west.

My older brother James, who is born near two years before me gave sound counsel regarding the perils of the decisions to be made. Having no surviving relatives other than James my brother and another brother Michael, still residing in Donegal in Ireland, it was decided the best option would be to head west where I would join the Union Pacific work crew, save my wages and buy a place of my own, God willing this come to pass, with the money I earn and save.

Should I perish and this account be found upon me, please forward to James McGlinchey, at Fitzwater Street, Philadelphia, Pennsylvania.

Fremont Nebraska - First Day

As I look out on this day, I wish my brother James could be here and see the look of the prairie. It is nothing at all like Philadelphia and I expect even less like Donegal in the old country even though I don't remember it at all. There is nothing but endless miles of grass in every direction and thankfully for our work crew, things are a bit flat making the prospect of quickly advancing the track westward more likely.

That may be the good news but I am not so sure my back and hands will hold long enough for me to make the whole way to California. The blisters on my hands from swinging a pick all day have broken. Up and down, up and down all the day. I can barely open my hands from clutching the handle all day. My back is sore and I am exhausted. The walking boss is on you quick enough if you slow the pace to a rate that causes him to notice. Several Swedes were thrown off the crew this afternoon because the foreman simply didn't like the sound of 'their gibberish' according to him.

Men from the both the Union and Confederate forces have made their way out here as many are still wearing the coats they had when they was fighting each other during the rebellion. Nobody has said nothing yet about it 'cause I expect each man needs the work and unlikely to start a fight this early in the building of the road. Still, I expect it won't take long 'til one or the other gets a bit of courage brought on by the drink and says something that will offend the other. Meself, I want no part of stepping into a fight that has already been settled but there are some who are not content to let well enough alone.

I expect I will need a new hat and boots soon enough because even though this land don't look too hard, the sun will wear a fellow out in no time at all. The boots I had since during the war are wearing out and I expect it would take a mighty gifted cobbler to keep these repaired all the way to California.

They have us sleeping in these specially built railroad cars with bunks stacked one on top of the other. I picked out one in the middle so that I don't have to sleep too low or too high but the down side is I look out when I wake up and see someone's arse staring me in the face. I guess you have to take the good with the bad.

This is all the energy I have to write for now.

JM

Dennis Quinn

A new man joined our crew today from County Wicklow that goes by the name of Dennis Quinn. He reminds me of my brother James with little tolerance for nonsense, whether it be from his work mates or his betters. He doesn't share a lot about himself and even though I would like to ask, 'taint none of me business.

A man carrying on that way is normal for men round these parts. Many of the lads are starting a new life and it is just as well in their mind to leave the old one behind so they don't care to spin yarns about the past. Another thing about Dennis that reminds me of James is his laugh which could shake the earth itself. He is a strong man that can do the work of two yet will only do so to help another man to keep the foreman off his back.

Dennis mentioned that he might care to head to Texas when all this is done but I am afraid that if he keeps up with the gambling the way he does, all he will have is the shirt on his back and long walk ahead of him. Still he is a capable man that is quick witted, good with numbers and afraid of nothing. Sometimes when he is digging, he'll spew out a line of Shakespeare, complete with the oratory gestures to the bewilderment of all around him and cause the walking boss to call down curses upon him. He will laugh that laugh of his, smile and pull his hat down around him and pitch another shovelful of dirt as though he hadn't a care in the world.

We are making great progress building little over a mile of track per day. It seems with the small army of men that we have working on this project we should be moving faster but there are so many obstructions to get past in this wilderness that on the balance of things, it is going quite well.

JM

Birthday

Today was my 20th birthday and it passed by uneventfully with an ordinary day of work filling grades and shoveling dirt with our crew. I didn't tell anyone about this being my birthday except my friends Quinn and a darky we call Hoppin' John. That's not his real name, it's just that a while back, he mixed up a batch of rice and black eyed peas the slaves used to eat and we asked him what it was. He told us that is was called Hop 'n Johns so of course he got the nickname Hopping John. His real name is Methuselah Elisha Claypool. The first two names are what his mammy named him and his Christian name belongs to his former master.

If the other men around here heard it was my birthday, they might contrive to get me over to the rolling town that is always camped nearby that is known as 'Hell on Wheels.' Every kind of vice imaginable occurs in this shanty town and it seems to attract every kind of evil Satan let loose on the planet. Men are murdered there nearly every day with their pockets picked cleaner than a chicken's neck.

We are making great progress on the construction of the road and haven't had any signs of Indians in quite a while. That is quite pleasing to Sgt. O'Halloran but he is not too hopeful this trend will continue. He and his men cut signs of many unshod Indian ponies not too long back and the buffalo hunters are shooting fewer and fewer of the beasts each time they go. This means to me the Indian will either have to submit to white authority or fight and I believe they will not submit on their own accord.

Let me get back to Hoppin' John. Even though he is a darky, he is a good man, one I am proud to have on my work crew. He easily stands over 6 feet 4 inches and is stout as a Virginia oak and could rival Finn McCool in size and strength. He can move more dirt than any two men on the crew. Even though he doesn't know how to read, he can recite verses from the Bible from memory with precise detail. Sometimes he tells me stories of West Africa that his Mammie told him when he was a little lad that are every bit as good as the ones Ma told of the little people, the Kings of Ireland, Cuchullain and such. Sometimes I read the newspaper to him and he sits there and comments on the events of the day with great insight into the character of the people. Many of the other work gangs berate him but I would rather him working with me than many of the drunken malcontents that come and go on others.

James mentioned in his last letter he was worried for me with all the wild Indians out in these parts attacking us but we are well guarded by the likes of Sgt. O'Halloran and his men that there is little cause for concern. I don't worry as I think wondering about the wrong quarter of Philadelphia at night is far more dangerous than this place.

JM

Nebraska Prairie – 1866

We are making great progress on the building the railroad as more workers come in each week from the East. They pile off the cars when they arrive, milling around and seem to be amazed at the desert they have found themselves in. Miles and miles of flat land, drying grass and a nearly treeless landscape provide no hindrance to the wind which blows across the land at amazing speed, bending the grass over in shimmering waves. Men from both the South and the North arrive but mostly they are countrymen who like us find it difficult to find work. Few speak of their origins as on more than one occasion it has led to a brawl and in one case a knife between the ribs when it was discovered a former Yankee soldier was bragging about his service at Shiloh within earshot of a Virginian who had lost his brother during the battle.

Tempers are often short here for many reasons, but mainly the long hours of backbreaking work in the intense heat. A man may receive a letter of bad news from home which will bring the bad spirit upon him. He may take to drinking and soon he will find hisself quarreling with another for no apparent reason. The railroad cars are reason enough to put a man in a foul mood with so many of us cramped in and barely room to turn around to put on your boots at the beginning of the day. I heard of one fellow who snored too much got the treatment. The other men of the car covered his face with a burlap bag and beat the tar out'a him. When I signed on to work this job, I was happy to learn that I would not have to sleep on the ground but now I do so on my own accord because of the stench of unwashed men, the noises they make tossing and turning, battling the demons in their sleep and the respite the cool earth provides.

The Casement brothers are running the work gangs here and some of the fellas get on with them while others don't at all. They are not the type to put up with any non-sense and expect strict obedience to their orders. Many of our countrymen do indeed struggle with this type of overbearing supervision, agreeing in person but cursing them beneath their breath once their back is turned. Better to work for a fair man such as this than an English landlord who never gave an even break to one of our own. Whatever you may feel about them, they are getting the job done as our work gangs are sometimes laying up 2 miles of track a day. Before you know it, we will find ourselves in California looking over the Pacific Ocean if we keep at it.

JM

Sgt. O'Halloran

Sgt. O'Halloran, a very dear man called on us today at our camp. A good Catholic to be sure, he brought a copy of the Philadelphia and New York newspapers for us to read which I did around the camp this evening for all who cared to listen.

He is also a very resourceful man and while he was talking to us atop his horse, a small herd of antelope were grazing off in the distance. He excused his self from our company and he and his roan loped off in the direction of the herd. Within a few minutes we heard the report of a Sharp's, a thunderous buffalo gun men use to hunt those beasts and shortly thereafter, returned with a fine doe for us to butcher for the feast that followed.

The meat surely did not taste like beef but considering the food that we have been eating these past six weeks, it was a welcome change.

This land is so wide open one can't imagine it and nothing at all like the Philadelphia or the old country. It was nothing like southern states that I saw either during the recent troubles. It is generally agreed upon by the men that this is not the desert it was made out to be from the rumors we heard when we first signed on to do the work.

Sgt. O'Halloran who remembers the old country much better than I, since I left we I was but a child agrees completely with the assessment. He often regales the fellas' and me with tales of the old country but reminds us that we are making tales of our own to share with our grandchildren some day.

'Tis true I am hoping but there remain some things to take care of in the mean time. With a bit of luck and saving my earnings, I will have land to raise cattle someday with a woman who'll have me.

JM

June 1866 - Columbus, Nebraska

The weather is turning quite nice now in this part of the world with the fields starting to green and the nights quite tolerable. A few days have passed warm enough to sleep with the doors open to allow the breeze to come in yet it is too early in the season for the mosquitoes or other pests to be bothering us yet.

We are making steady progress on the work, ever moving westward but many obstacles remain. If you were to listen to our foremen, you would think we were making no progress at all. Still, the truth I suspect lies somewhere in the middle because to be sure there are many mountains and rivers to overcome. It seems we have some very clever men on hand to beat whatever obstacle is placed in front of us though.

Today I got my first sight of an Indian. It was not at all like you might think that you hear about with the whooping war party and the painted faces but a wretched figure the likes you have never seen. Sgt. O'Halloran and his men were out patrolling the area when they came across the woman who dismissed all pretense of stoicism that the redskins are inclined to show and waved at his patrol frantically for attention. The sergeant was wary of this at first, as his experience was such that it might be a prelude to an ambush and proceeded cautiously toward the woman running their direction.

The woman was covered in soot and her hair filled with grasses, having been alone in the prairie for over a week, drinking from buffalo wallows and eating whatever roots she could find. After some deliberation, it was determined the woman was an escaped captive from the Sioux tribe who had been carried off during a raid from her own tribe of Pawnee some four and half years earlier. She further explained a freak lightning storm had set the prairie on fire and she used the opportunity to escape her captors as they fled in every direction to evade the catastrophe.

Once in our camp, antelope steak, beans and potatoes were offered which she accepted with no reservation and in no time at all, the plate was empty and she was licking the bottom to clean the gravy.

The appearance of this woman made something clear to me that is true no matter who or where you are and it is this. Freedom is not a gift to be taken lightly whether it be among the heathen or the tenants back in County Donegal. Maybe with the good Lord's blessings, our countrymen will have theirs one day.

JM

A Dog Comes to Camp

Today a dog came to our camp and began sniffing around. I didn't pay her much mind because a lot of people from the shantytowns and the settlers heading west bring their dogs with them and I figured once she got tired of sniffing around, she would head back to her master.

This was an ugly dog for sure, with black and grey striped hair, spotted brown near her stomach and ears that flop around whenever she lopes from one spot to another looking for food. She was long legged and lean, though quite nimble as one of the men picked up a rock to throw at her to chase her off but she dodged it easily.

She came trotting over my direction and when she got around me, took a long look at me and started sniffing my way. Directly she began wagging her tail and let her tongue hang loose as if she was waiting for me to tell her something.

"What you want girl?" I asked her. She sat down on her hind legs just looking at me and watching every movement I was making. I thought she might be hungry so I took out a piece of beef jerky I had wrapped up in my pocket in case I got hungry before dinner time and pulled off a slice. Soon as I had that piece out of my pocket, the dog stood up on her hind legs as I threw the slice over to her. She easily caught it in mid-air and swallowed it nearly whole and looked to me again for another.

"Uh-oh," said Quinn. "Looks like you found you a new friend, McGlinchey."

"I reckon I have at that," says I.

I peeled off another piece and threw the piece way high in the air. The dog eyed it and placed herself right under the arc of the throw and caught the meat in mid-air. Wagging her tail, she came over to show her appreciation for my generosity and sat on her hind legs in front of me. Holding her right paw out as if to shake hands, she waited for me to grab her paw and move it up and down. Not wanting to appear unfriendly, I squatted down on my haunches to do just that. The dog shook my hand and moved into me, licking my hands and folding his ears back showing me she wanted to be petted.

Like all dogs, they appreciate good ear scratching and I commenced to scratching her behind the ears and on her backside to which she seemed intent on not letting me stop. She arched her back, moved into me this way and that just to get the right angle on the scratching.

Soon my hand grew tired of scratching this gal and I told her to go on. She looked at me kind of confused as if she didn't know what I was saying. She moved off a ways and I picked up a small stick and threw it at her but missed on purpose, just so she would get the idea that I wanted her to move on back to her master.

The girl ran down the stick and picked it up between her jaws and brought it back to me, tail a wagging.

"My goodness," says I. "This dog can fetch as well."

I threw the stick again and again and the dog ran after it as many times as I threw it and returned it to me. Well, a dog that works that hard deserves a reward so I pulled out the rest of my jerky and threw it to her on the ground and she gobbled it up in two bites. I then began looking for a basin to fill with water and as soon as I found one that was suitable, went to the barrel and poured out a few cups into it.

I placed it on the ground and she drank it dry. She didn't bother looking up until it was nearly empty so I gave her a couple of more cups and she almost finished that.

I reached down to pet her and said I have to go in and sleep because I have to work tomorrow. "Go back to your master," says I but she just stayed nearby watching me go in the sleeping car.

If she is still here tomorrow with no master to come looking for her, I shall name her Colleen, which means 'little girl' in the Irish.

JM

Colleen becomes my dog

This morning I rolled out of bed as normal and went to stand in the doorway of the dormitory car to see what kind of day it was shaping up to be. The sun was already over the horizon and I reached for the ceiling, giving myself a good stretch to get all the kinks out of my body. I could smell the food cooking down in the dining car and I was hungry from the smell. Already there was the clanking of metal being hit against metal, horses pulling wagons The noise in the camp was always non-stop it seemed with all the people talking and machinery moving.

As I was putting my suspenders over my shoulders, I saw a black shape emerge from under the car and trotted out from underneath. Wagging her tail, that dog I had fed yesterday looked at me and was waiting for me to come down so she could greet me.

"Good morning," says I to my new friend. "I hope you slept well in spite of these modest accommodations."

As I walked down the ramp, the girl came over to me and nudged my hand with her nose so I would pet her. I bent down and gave her a little scratch behind the ears and stood up directly and began walking toward the dining car. As I got to the line, I knew the cook was not going to stand for any dog coming inside so I pointed and gave her the command, "Go lie down."

Sure enough, that dog went underneath the car and lay down with her paws crossed one over the top of the other and watched me go inside.

16

After I had a bite to eat, I came outside again and the dog was still there waiting for me. I told her to "Stay," which she did and lay down in the same position again, waiting for me to come back. I went to the back of the car where the cook's helpers were cutting up beef and preparing the huge amount of food to feed all these men.

"Good morning to you," says I.

"And to yourself," they returned.

"I seem to have made a friend in the way of a dog that has attached herself to me. I was wondering if you fellows would do me a kindness as well as be interested in making an extra four bits a week by putting aside the parts of the steer you would be throwing away and saving it for me to feed this dog. I will come around every day to collect some spare scraps of meat that you put aside. Is it a deal?"

"Sure, sure," says one fellow who seem good natured indeed. "I like dogs meself and I could sure use the extra money. Here is a piece for her now and come back when you need some more. We got plenty we throw away and it don't seem likely we will run out."

"I thank you for your kindness," says I. Taking the piece of meat in my hand, I started walking back toward the car that Colleen was laying under. She began wagging her tail as I got closer but did not move until I called her out from underneath the car.

This dog was a wonder and it seemed she understood every word I was telling her. She obediently sat and knew a treat was coming her way. I threw the piece of meat up in the air and she leaped up at it, grabbing it and pulling it down. She held it in her mouth and dropped it to the ground and began eating it in gulps but not nearly with the same vigor she did the previous night.

"All right girl," says I. "Now go chase a rabbit or something. Off to work I go. Now behave yourself and I will give you another when I return."

Sure enough, off she went into the prairie looking for something but I don't know what. I turned my back and looked over my shoulder a time or two until I lost sight of her. She would be back, I was sure. How I was going to keep this dog I was not so sure.

JM

A letter from my brother

I received a letter today from my brother James today along with the Philadelphia newspaper and it was greatly appreciated. It seems the city is growing at rate I can't even imagine with new construction spreading out in every direction. From the sounds of it, the Irish are coming out of the ground like ants from their mound.

James mentioned overhearing some of the new arrivals speaking the Irish when he was walking home from the work day.

There are few on the crew here who speak it amongst themselves, mostly from the west part of the old country and fewer who understand the gist of the conversation. The foreman gets riled if he hears any of the work crew going on for any length of time in another language but he can do nothing about it when we are camped for the evening as we have few visitors outside of our own group.

It seems the Irish are filling up the whole country and willing to do just about anything to earn a living. Our foreman is constantly reminding us of the fact that if we don't perform there be thousands of the Irish waiting to take our job. I expect the same is true in Philadelphia as well with our countrymen looking for work with many in the factories that are springing up all around the city. While I don't blame a person for getting work where he finds it, I can't see myself coming back and doing that. I will save my money and give more thought to it.

Holding your money is especially hard 'round these parts with all the low life waiting to relieve you of any that you have. Just the other day, a fellow by the name of Foley and some of his crew came to our sleeping car to look for a fellow that he says owes him money. The crew is a bad lot and apparently he is lending some of the lads money for the drink and charging them interest that is hard to pay back. Soon enough, many will be earning their wages to pay him rather than themselves.

JM

Platte River

Today is Sunday and I thought I would go down to the Platte to cool off because of the heat. As I was sitting under a shade tree, a man and two of the fattest whores I ever saw came down to the river for a skinny dip. The party was having a grand old time splashing about, laughing and carrying on in a delightful way. I couldn't decide between gouging out me own eyes or moving on to another site to take my nap. Even though I was tired, I decided it would be better to move.

JM

Kearny Nebraska, August 1866

The Catholic gangs have been extra busy this week but not for swinging a sledge, moving dirt or laying track on the prairie. News that Father Ryan of Columbus, a town a few miles back up the way will come to the camp to administer the sacraments and hold mass for the crews according to Mr. Casement. The men cheered when they heard the news because our faith is one the cornerstones of our Irish identity and many a man here has a lot to talk about when the priest goes to hearing confession. The Ulster Presbyterians and other Protestants didn't show any interest in the event. These fellows we work with don't begrudge us our faith unlike other parts of the country that have a thorough dislike for our kind.

A large tent has been strung and staked and you would think the pope hisself was a coming by all the preparations that are going into mass. Cottonwood railroad ties, which are a comfort to sit on by the way, are being stacked quite neatly to make a place for the men to set when Father Ryan arrives. I myself have been practicing the vespers and trying to recite the little bit of Latin I remember when Ma used to make us attend the mass back in Philadelphia. I didn't do so well but Dennis Quinn who I spoke of previously from County Wicklow has a memory of an elephant and could recite the mass from beginning to end in Latin and Greek. Mind you, he did so not to blaspheme but I think as a bit of showin' off and to help those like myself who have a hard time remembering our prayers. Dennis says he will be joining me at the mass because although he has a glib heart, deep down I believe there is something he is dragging around inside of him that he needs to get off his chest. Going to confession with Father Ryan and reciting the rosary two or three times might be just the thing for him.

Hoppin' John don't go in for anything so tame as the "Catholic way of praising da' Lawd," as he likes to put it. Some of him and his darky friends get together on Saturday nights off a ways from the rest of us and begin to hollerin and shouting praises to the Lord. I was out walking the prairie one Saturday evening when an itinerant Negro preacher who I did not recognize was out in a clearing with a campfire and torches a burning. You could barely make out the dark shapes of the men dancing around the

21

fire, clapping their hands and singing praises to Jesus. The preacher's voice kept getting louder and louder, talking about the saving grace of Jesus and will you be there in heaven with Jesus and I can't hear you say it brother and drive the devil out of this place by clapping your hands and singing praise to Jesus. Let me tell you, I never seen nothing like it in my 20 years on this earth and it scared me a bit in one way and was sort of amusing in another. Hoppin' John, a big serious man was right there with them, clapping his hands and singing praises to Jesus. Later on when he returned to camp, he didn't say a thing about the meeting but he seemed very relaxed in his demeanor.

I will write more after Father Ryan's visit.

JM

Father Ryan's mass

Today Father Ryan came from Columbus and ministered the mass to the men. General Jack is a pretty fair man when it comes to letting the men off to rest for the Sabbath even if most of the men carry on like it was any other day, drinking, gambling and buying all manner of goods.

Today was different however and most of the lads attended the mass and held the day as a holy one. Father Ryan held the confessional several hours before the mass and I expect his ears were red from all the sin he was called on to absolve that day. Long lines were assembled outside of the Father's tent and there was a lot of sin for these fellows to account for. Rosaries would be worn clean down to nubby little beads if the men finished their penance according to Father Ryan's direction.

Anyway, we sang some of the favorite hymns that every Catholic knows and for sure you could hear the Irish brogue among the voices lifted up to heaven that day. Many a man has a wonderful voice, some that could sing baritone in an opera if they had a mind to, sang the hymns that would bring tears to your eyes. The father recited the mass in Latin and surprisingly, most of the men could answer back in the ancient language.

Soon, it came time for the sermon and Father Ryan asked us all to sit and we took our place on the cottonwood ties.

Father Ryan started off telling us how difficult it would be for a good Catholic to keep his soul from being marked black as Satan's with so much temptation surrounding us and every vice known to man thrust our direction. But God never allows us a temptation we can not defeat. It was our duty as Catholics to do the best job at our chosen occupation that we can, restrain from the drink and loose women and to save our money so that we may be of some value to our families after this is all done. "You are on a great mission and diluting your strength by giving in to vice does not serve your fellow man, your country, the Holy Church or your God," he emphasized with a slap of his hand into his open palm.

He closed the mass with a benediction and afterward, the men stopped by to thank the Father for coming all the way out here to minister to us. "Keep faithful to the Holy Church, boys," he offered as encouragement. "Recite your rosaries," and "Pray to the Holy Family to keep you from sin," he added over and over until the crowd of men finally dwindled away.

I thanked him as well and greatly appreciated his sermon. He met with General Jack and Mr. Dan Casement who both thanked him for his time and I believe gave him a special offering for the poor and for a new vessel for his church. He boarded the train to return East and the men lifted their hats to wave goodbye. He kept making the sign of the cross over us and waving from the rear platform as his car slowly disappeared. "God bless you boys," he shouted toward us. "Stay true to the Holy Church," and "Pray your rosaries," until we could hear him no more.

Soon the train was over the horizon with only a thin wisp of black smoke to show that Father Ryan had been here. The men broke away from the track in random groups, staring at the track and looking about to see the transformation that was but a passing phase. The connection we had was once again gone and the camp returned to the state it was before.

The Comstock

Many of the lads in the camp are buzzing with the news of silver in Nevada. Rumor has it that the Irish lads are leaving the Central Pacific side and heading for the fields hoping to make their fortune. I must admit that I am a bit tempted myself to make a go of it but in my mind, I know it is a fool's errand. If history is any judge of who will get rich from the strike it will not be the poor Irish gandy dancers but the likes of Governor Stanford, Charles Crocker and so forth. No, I believe the smart money will be those that sell the shovels, supply the cattle and sad to say, the whiskey which will keep the lads working for next to near subsistence.

I have no desire to see my life shortened in a mine accident. If the men who work the mines are like anything here, they must be ever vigilant for those who handle the powder since they often set off the explosions without a thought for those who are nearby, giving little to no warning of their activities. Worse yet, those who are lost in accidents are replaced with new men and quickly forgotten by those who hire their labor.

Many men talk of leaving to go this place or that place when we finish the project but I don't see how they will do it. Drinking and gambling and all manner of vice are the constant companions of camps where there are no women to add any civilizing effect. Our pay is given us and there are precious few men that have a penny to their name a week after the paymasters' car has returned to Omaha. Thankfully, with the help of the Lord and my prayers of intercession to the Virgin Mary, I am one of the exceptions to this sad trend of our Irish brethren and managed to save most of my wages so far. At last count, I had 278 dollars which I keep close by in my purse.

I can't see how any Irishman would not wish to own his own place when you think we are not permitted to own land in our own country unless we are willing to forsake the Holy Church and swear allegiance to the Anglicans. It makes no matter to me what faith a man subscribes to but I don't believe it should be a requirement to own property. Luckily, the great men like Benjamin Franklin and Thomas Jefferson agreed with me and now I may get a place that I can call my own.

JM

Plum Creek, Nebraska – A Pinkerton Arrives

A stranger rode into our work site today and ended up turning the place upside down, even worse than the Indian raids affect the men. At first glance, there was nothing unusual about him except he was eyeing the men awfully close for a stranger and seemed to be looking for somebody. Nobody usually pays us much mind as they are most often looking for Mr. Dan or General Jack or one of the fellows who keeps track of the supplies. This fellow was different in that he was wearing a short brimmed hat and his face was sun burned. This fellow for sure didn't do much outside work by the look of him. He was rather short and clean shaven. The clothes were mostly clean, much cleaner than those of the men around here which means it ain't been too long since he was in a town and had his laundry done.

He came riding up to Mr. Dan and started speaking with him directly who then called over one of the foremen. The fellow thought for a second and then pointed out toward our direction. The stranger came riding over to where a group of men were digging to pile dirt for a grade and he came up behind a fellow they call Jack Parnell.

"Are you Jack Finley?" the man asks Jack.

"So who is asking, if you would be polite enough to identify yourself," Jack replies.

"My name is Cannady," says the stranger. "And I have a writ for your arrest for bank robbery in Ohio."

"You have the wrong Finley," says Jack. "I have never set foot in Ohio."

Cannady threw down some leg irons and hand restraints. He glared at Finley and with no waiver in his voice said, "Put these on... slowly."

"I am telling you mister, I ain't never been to Ohio," says Jack.

About this time, Jack's brother addresses Cannady as well and says, "Mister, you have the wrong man. My brother here tain't never been to Ohio or have I. We got off the boat in New Orleans and made our way west."

"You two come from County Wicklow, in the old country don't you?" says Cannady.

"Aye, we do but what's that got to do with the price of tea in China?" says Sean Finley.

"Well I got business with you too...This is the last time I'm going to tell you. Put those leg irons and hand restraints on. Don't matter who wears which. Just put 'em on."

"We will not," says Sean. "We demand to know who you..."

Before Sean could say another word, Cannady had pulled his gun from his holster and leveled it at Sean. He fired one ball into his chest, leaving a billowing cloud of black smoke to fill the air. As Sean fell backward, he put another in his forehead.

We were all stunned at the shot as was Jack no less. Cannady's horse reared but Jack didn't move as his jaw slackened in disbelief. His eyes followed his brother's fall to the ground and he looked with horror at Cannady's stoic, mechanistic demeanor.

As the roan's front feet alit, Cannady turned toward Jack and shot him in the eye socket, causing the side of his head to explode. Jack crumpled into a ball on the ground with a pool of blood draining around his body.

Gazing at the men from this horse, Cannady was satisfied his work was done. He turned his reins back toward Mr. Dan and asked if he might buy a couple of horses to take his bounties back to the rail station. Mr. Dan agreed, seemingly stunned as the next person. "Get a couple of horses ready for Mr. Cannady," he told the foreman.

About that time I got my wits about me and could talk again. "**Jesus, Joseph and Mary,**" says I. "What was that all about?" I shouted to Quinn.

"It was an execution," says Quinn. "Those fellows never were in Ohio, just like they said. This Cannady is a Pinkerton who got some judge in Ohio to sign a writ or got someone to forge it to make it look real. Those boys were Fenians, wanted back in the old country for doing something against the English. Somebody must have told where they were and a bounty was put out for 'em. No matter now, the Finley brothers are dead."

"Now how would you be knowing this?" say I.

"Because I belong to the brotherhood, meself," whispers Quinn.

At that, I said no more for the rest of the day. I didn't want any ears listening that didn't need to be knowing things not their concern.

JM

The Day after the Finley Brothers' Killing

My friend Quinn revealed something to me when he came back from Shantytown that did not at all surprise me. He had a couple of whiskeys with the lads and he was not at all at a loss of his faculties. He felt needed to unburden himself with something that's been on his conscience.

Before laboring on the railroad, Dennis and his family was farming a plot of land that had not been feeding his mother and eight other family members. Dennis was the second eldest and he was often called upon to look for wage work, no matter the length of employ, so the family could pay their obligations. One day while he was walking down the lane returning home after an unsuccessful day of looking for work, he hears a coach rambling and clattering toward him from behind. "Clear the way, clear the way, clear the way," the coachman shouted toward him. The lanes in Ireland are so narrow however there was no place to move except into the hedge. Dennis squeezes himself up against the hedge as tight as he can with just a matter of inches between him, the horses and the carriage to the front of him and hedge to the back of him.

No sooner had the coach passed did it stop with the landlord of the estates jumping out of the carriage demanding to know why Dennis did not remove his hat to show his respect when he passed. Dennis' temper by this time was starting to grow within him and it is a sight to be feared for those not knowing him. Dennis starts to get sassy with him asking him if it is only Englishmen who have eyes in their 'arses' and can see through their pants or did he think the Irish were equipped by God in the same manner. Worse yet, he held the landlord's gaze and made no attempt to calm the situation. By this time, both tempers are up and the landlord tells the coachman to beat Dennis with the whip to teach him a lesson. Well, Dennis is having none of this and he grabs the whip from the coachmen and gives him a taste of his own medicine. The coachman who according to Dennis is a thin undertaker looking sort of fellow runs off down the road to fetch the constable.

Dennis then turns his attention to the landlord who is backing away not believing his eyes. He turns to run but Dennis picks up a rock and throws it at him, hitting him in the back of the head and knocking him down. He walks over and stands over him with the whip and begins to beat the living daylights out of him. After four or five times, striking him across the face Dennis begins to beat on him with his fist. The landlord swings back at him but is no match for Dennis who has got the devil's own fury in him by this time. Dennis knocks some of his teeth out and breaks his jaw, leaving the now unconscious man bloody and beaten.

Dennis is starting to get his wits about him again and starts to understand the trouble he has put himself in. He runs all the way home and tells his family what has happened. Packing what clothes he has, he travels across the field by night to Dublin to catch the ferry to Liverpool and then a ship to America.

One thing that in all the excitement he forgot that started it all was his hat. Dennis let his hat behind in the lane where he left the landlord and the constabulary put out a 25 £ reward for anybody who could identify the owner of the hat. Well, with that kind of money and Irish being as poor as they are, it didn't take long for someone to finger Dennis but he was long gone by this time. But that didn't stop the landlord for taking out his vengeance against him because he came with some men one day, scars still on his face where Dennis had put them and had his family turned off the land. He and his men torched their home and they were left out in the lane with only the clothes on their back.

Dennis' family has written him and told them they are waiting in Liverpool, hoping to catch a ship to America. Dennis is saving his money and hoping to send some to them so they can make their way to Philadelphia or New York and find some work. He has saved $97 so far but that is not enough to bring everyone. He will probably send a little bit now and have the oldest come first so they can earn enough money to send home for their mother and young ones.

By this time, Dennis is getting emotional and talking a bit loud, feeling the guilt for the predicament his family is in.

"Quiet," says I. "You don't know who might be listening to us and turning you in for the reward money."

Dennis returns to his story in a whisper loud enough for any who wish to hear in the next sleeping car. Trying to get a man with the drink to be quiet is difficult but they never seem to know just how loud they are. About this time I am getting the feeling someone is indeed listening to us 'cause the normal noises have stopped. I walk over to the door and look out and there a few yards away is Foley and his crew. They look my way but don't say nothing. I don't know if they heard or not but by this time Dennis has already crawled into his bunk with all his clothes on and is snoring.

JM

Henry Morton Stanley

Today a Welsh newspaper reporter came out to the work site with General Jack to write about the work that is going on. He said his name was Henry Morton Stanley and he asked a whole lot of questions about the goings on here. He walked throughout the site chatting with all the men. When he came to me, he shook my hand and turned it over to look at all the calluses. "That's the hardest hand I ever shook," says he.

"Not surprising, sir," says I. "Every man here could dig to China with one hand and throw a bull in another," I joked in return.

Mr. Stanley has a natural way with people and made himself well liked among the men right away. Soon as he had a small crowd about him he began talking about all the 'to-do' people back East are making about this railroad, the fear people have of the Indians and his travels among the soldiers while they go looking for those who are murdering and harassing the workers. He asked us what we thought about 'Hell on Wheels', a term Mr. Stanley borrowed from another newspaperman for the shantytown that follows us wherever we go. "There is no absence of vice in that place," Mr. Stanley declared, letting us know his feelings for the place. "It seems all the filth of humanity has made its way West and follow along behind you like a dust cloud," he added.

General Jack arranged a show of our abilities so Mr. Stanley's readers would get an idea how things were coming along on the prairie. At a pre-arranged signal, the general gave the walking boss a nod and we commenced to laying the rails at a speed we only go for people the General and Mr. Dan want to impress. Off we went with the men shouting 'Down' to drop the rail. Another would come along and position it on the tie with others still behind to drive the spikes in three strikes of the hammer. We laid a 700 feet of track in a matter of a few minutes and Mister Stanley show his appreciation for the show by clapping his hands and tipping his hat to the men exclaiming in a loud voice that "the rails shall soon be in the Pacific in no time if we continue with the zeal we have shown here."

To a man we were exhausted by the show we put on but it made General Jack's chest swell out so much that the buttons pretty near popped off his coat. Anyway, he gave us double our daily pay for our efforts and bit of tobacco. I got no use for the tobacco but it is good to trade with the other men who are partial to it.

Mr. Stanley soon rode off with Mr. Dan and General Jack promising to return soon to check on our progress.

JM

100th Meridian – The Big Wigs go for a Buffalo Hunt

General Jack and Mr. Dan told us that some men would be coming out to celebrate our big achievement of reaching the hundredth meridian. I don't know what that means to most folks, but to us, it is a line on a map that we can't see and don't care about neither. One bit of prairie looks pretty much the same on either side of the line but if they want to throw a party to celebrate, who are we to argue?

Because of that, some of the big wigs from New York came out west to see how their investments were doing. It seems that these fellas are the ones who helped put together the money involved and solicited others to invest in the building of the railroad along with their cronies in Congress.

They got off at the last station where there was a place to disembark and were met by General Jack, Mr. Dan, and whole bunch of Army types including Sgt. O'Halloran who had to trail along to make sure these fellas didn't get in any trouble.

They arrived at the camp and walked around a bit with General Jack showing them the progress that was being made and how the work was done and so forth. These men seemed right polite and didn't interfere in none of the work we was doing, just looked around and took it all in. One of them commented how horrible the landscape looked and we ought to let the savages have the whole of this wretched place, just build the railroad through it as quick as we could. I reckon he was the most truthful of the bunch 'cause the others just laughed and looked at him like they hoped he was making a joke. "You couldn't pay me to take a section of land out here," he was ranting on while the others laughed politely.

Anyway, Sgt. O'Halloran's superiors set up a buffalo hunt for these fellows and it was clear from the beginning they were out of their element. These Wall Street dandies didn't know nothing about riding a horse, much less how to shoot a gun. The whole time one or the other was letting the reins slap their horse on the neck or another would be holding them too tight confusing the horse as to what his intent was. Most of the party rode in a hospital wagon that the Army lent so these men could ride out into the prairie to do their hunt with some Pawnee scouts along to look for a herd to steer their direction. Each of the men was given a Sharps .50 caliber rifle and off they went in pursuit of their game.

Before long the Pawnee scouts returned telling the Sergeant they had spotted a small herd of about 100 buffalo over the rise and they would try to steer them back this direction. Off the scouts went with some of the Wall Street fellas on horseback loping over the prairie. As soon as they got to the rise, they galloped straight toward the herd, not knowing how much damage one of those things can do to a horse or a man. One of the fellas fell off of his horse when his horse stepped in a prairie dog hole so Major North, Sgt. O'Halloran's commanding officer took off after him to make sure he was all right. Sure enough, the Major's horse lost his footing in a hole as well and threw him. Both of them was pretty badly bruised but not seriously injured.

It was a good thing the herd was heading the opposite direction or the two of them would have gotten a lot more beat up than that. Anyway, one of the Pawnee scouts cut out a bunch of buffalo and started heading them toward the hospital wagon where the rest of the New Yorkers were riding. He got them close enough to where they could get in some good shots and the wagon started opening up on the unfortunate buffalo and dropped three of them.

The men stopped their wagon and got out to inspect their kills. They were mighty proud of their shooting and kept recounting the tale amongst each other about who did what, who fired which shot that dropped which buffalo, marveling at the size of the beast and so on. You could say these fellows were full of themselves and thought they could do anything even though the Pawnee scout is the one who really deserves the credit.

Before they headed back to camp, Sgt. O'Halloran overheard the New Yorkers asking the Major if it wouldn't be too much trouble to seek out and engage the Sioux in a battle. The Cheyenne would do if the Sioux were not available and they continued on in the most serious manner of what the Major's opinion of the prospects to shoot at some enemy warriors that day.

When I heard that I durn near spit out my coffee. "They said what?!" I said to O'Halloran.

"You heard me right, boy-oh," the Sergeant said. "I couldn't believe it meself and thankfully the Major made his apologies about how the Sioux would not be making themselves available that day on account of there was the annual hunt they would concerning themselves with as well as the full moon preventing any self-respecting Sioux from fighting the white man when they had to dance around their campfire all night."

Satisfied with that answer, the big wigs started back for the station, continuing in their bragging of who shot which buffalo, how they stared down the beast through the sights of their gun and the steady nerves which pulled the trigger which dropped the animal to the ground. Returning once again to their domains to which they are best suited, they boarded their rail car to return east and continue their stories of their great hunt out West.

JM

North Platte River – November 1866

Work is becoming more tolerable as the season begins to change around us. The skies are turning more cloudy and overcast with the wind whipping over the prairie almost constantly. One good thing about it is we have barely time to sweat before the wind sweeps it away keeping us comfortable while we labor throughout the day. Sleeping at night is getting uncomfortable and I have returned to the rolling dormitories when it is time to lie down for the evening.

Our gang witnessed an unusual sight today. We were making enough racket to wake the dead themselves with the clanging of metal, the squeaking of wagons, men cursing, when a sound overhead caught our attention. A flock of geese were moving in a V formation southward, honking at each other and flapping their wings, laboring with the most serious of intentions. Luckily for them the wind was behind them and they seemed quite happy not to be fighting to make their way to warmer climates. Hoppin' John turned his holey hat up to shield the sun from his eyes muttering 'Lawd have mercy, Lawd have mercy, Lawd have mercy' over and over. The whole crew looked up toward the skies and work on the rails fell silent as the hardest of men marveled at God's creation. Even the walking bosses or Mr. Casement it is reported from the men didn't say a word of rebuke 'cause he himself was looking up at the birds and admiring the sight, with a broad grin over his face. Soon, the worker's returned to their duties with the hammering and beating of the ground with occasional scans toward the sky to see if any new flocks might come our way.

Because winter will soon be upon us, they are increasing our work quotas and from what I hear, the snow can get up to the height of a man here on the prairie. Mr. Casement's foremen are always to be seen on every part of the track urging the men to work harder, cursing those that fall behind, which as you might imagine, has little effect on an Irishman due to the wide stubborn streak our countrymen have. Some of the men are organizing in groups to discuss the conditions of our work, how much we are to be paid and so forth. I can tell you for sure, when a man knows he has several months wages coming to him, some lads feel they are richer than the Solomon himself and will behave in the most insubordinate manner if it gives another a laugh and builds himself up at the expense of the foreman.

When the ground becomes too difficult to break, we expect to stop work until it thaws. What all these men are going to do to keep themselves busy during the winter is anyone's guess however General Dodge and those Wall Street dandies have not sought me out to ask my advice. I expect we will have more time on our hands as there is not much daylight and too many hours to fill just looking over the prairie. Wherever we are and whatever we are doing, I am hoping to stay warm.

Nebraska – Winter, 1867

I am very bored today. The recent snowstorms have left the ground very hard and the howling wind makes any person that steps outside appear like a staggering drunk. General Jack Casement has told the crews he doesn't know when we will begin working again because it all depends on the weather but I would much rather work in the cold than sit inside doing nothing. The General has taken the train back to Omaha to talk over the situation with the higher ups.

We have plenty to eat but it is generally the same thing over and over. Meat, bread and beans, meat, bread and beans, meat, bread and beans. One good thing about the weather is the men don't sweat as much and therefore don't smell nearly so. On the other hand, the beans make the men fart something awful and you can wake up in the middle of the night thinking you are being suffocated by the amount gas passed in the sleeping quarters.

Men have been playing endless rounds of cards, telling ghost stories from the old country or getting drunk, mostly getting drunk. Boredom and drunkenness usually go hand in hand on the frontier and men will do just about anything to make them forget their situation or do something to make the time go faster. General Jack has a low tolerance for drunkards and the drink but looks the other way if a man doesn't make a nuisance of himself and bother the others. If someone gets out of hand, a friend of the man will usually take care of him but sometimes that's not enough. He may pick a fight with the wrong person and end up getting the tar beat out of him or if he is unlucky to be by himself, worse. Men die here all the time either from sickness or getting murdered and it doesn't pay to not have a friend looking out for you in either situation.

I make it point to never go out to buy something by myself in the little shantytowns that are ever springing up on the side of the work camps. Every low character in this country seems to have emerged and set up shop in these places. One fellow on my work gang went to buy some tobacco and a bottle of whiskey for he and his friends to share and never returned. His friends wondering what had become of him went looking for him and found him facedown behind a row of tents with a stab wound in his back and his pockets gone through. No one had seen or heard nothing with this man's killer never to be found.

Dennis or Hoppin' John and me always go together if we need something or just want to stretch the legs and look at the new fangled things that are making their way West. The soiled doves are always shouting at us to come into their tent to show us something, whiskey peddlers a free sample, gamblers a square game, a man selling medicine to cure anything that ails you. The buildings go up and come down at these places so fast that General Grant's quartermasters could not match the speed at which these people set up shop. Stores are anything from two barrels with a board set up over the top of it to wooden buildings with fancy wooden floors and lights that go on at night.

One thing you have to say about this railroad is it has increased the speed of commerce unlike any other place or time in history. You could buy some fruit in Philadelphia and carry it with you all the way to Nebraska before it has time to spoil. The same can be said for the merchandise of the people who set up their businesses here. It is an amazing time that we live in.

JM

Ghost stories

I had the scare of my life yesterday evening but it is nothing like you might imagine with Indians on the war path or buffalo stampedes.

Some of the fellas' from the old country, particularly those from the western islands like the Blaskets were sitting about a fire telling tales of the spirits that walked the bogs looking for souls to steal in times long ago. Well, these fellas's were going on about the vengefulness of one spirit in particular, describing it in the Irish that it was sure to put a chill up the spine of any a person who had ears and could understand our language. Just when the ghost was about to carry off the person into the netherworld who should come up behind me but Sgt. O'Halloran screaming like a banshee and masked with an old white sheet. I very nearly fell over meself scrambling to escape the grip of Lucifer when the laughter of the men brought me back to me senses.

I had a good mind to have a go at the Sergeant but couldn't bring myself to do it, he being such a fine man and me showing myself not able to take a little joke such as that. Still, when I turned in that evening, I made sure to look all around before I covered myself.

The following day, some drovers came by the camp and I recognized one of them, a lad from my old outfit that used to drive cattle to the troops during the war. His name was Jack Pearsall from Harrisburg and we sat down and chatted awhile, catching up on the latest bit of news. What a small world isn't it? Anyway, Jack told me he was heading down Texas way because there was a lot of land available for a person who was willing to work hard and save his money to buy a bit of land. Good land for grazing cattle and with the cities like Philadelphia filling up with people from the old country, a cattle man could make a pretty fair living.

Land is something I would very much like to have once this is over with but I don't rightly know where I would like to settle. The Comanches are pretty much whipped in Texas and it seems like a good place to run a herd if the grass is as good as Jack says it is. Anyway, I have no more time to be thinking about that for now as I must get to my cot with a long day looking my way in the morrow.

JM

Platte River

The Army and the Union Pacific have come upon a grand idea to gain influence with the Pawnee nation. Good I say because one less tribe attacking our work gangs is one less enemy to worry about.

Pawnee Indian braves are to be employed as scouts for the U.S. Army helping track down the Cheyenne and Sioux tribes who have been killing our workmen and stealing our livestock. It is even worse for some of the Mormons and other settlers who have been heading west getting caught out in the open with no one but themselves to defend against the brutality of these ruthless warriors.

Not that the red man can be blamed because the railroad means the end of their way of life. I don't intend to offer my scalp however to diminish their anger.

Of course, many times survivors of an attack claim they was Indians when it really was white men dressed up as Indians to steal their livestock. Some of these folks back East have never seen an Indian and wouldn't know one if they was to stand up right next to one.

The Pawnee are a good group of Indians however and this makes sense. They are the natural enemies of the Sioux and when they were asked if they would like to earn some money fighting the Sioux, they thought they had died and gone to the happy hunting ground or wherever an Indian goes when he dies. These fellas' are good fighters and they ain't like a lot of that are always trying to steal or get a quart of whiskey to get drunk on. Heck, even that squaw that Sgt. O'Halloran brought in from the prairie pitches in and helps out. She has been doing some of the washing and cooking for the soldiers and I ain't heard one of 'em yet complaining about it. She don't say much 'cause I expect she don't know much English. As far as the braves go, I have never seen one Pawnee pick up the bottle and starting acting like a jackass like many of the other tribes do.

Even though most of the men around here have taking a liking to the Pawnee, they still have some fun with them.

Just the other day, several Pawnee families came in to camp to pick up some supplies, beef and such that the company and Army gives the braves for scouting. A train was idling on the track and old men, women, children, squaws were climbing through the engine, over the coal car, touching the wheels not really sure what to make of it all. An ornery Welsh engineer by the name of Griffith took note of all the attention paid by the newcomers and decided to have a bit of fun with the party. Without warning, the Welshman gave a long tug on the whistle lanyard sending out a shrill screech that would wake Lazarus. At the same time, he sent a column of steam to the sides of the engine blowing a cloud of hot mist over the scrambling Pawnee families. Indians came pouring out of every side of the engine, young and old, sprinting as fast as they could away from the belching iron behemoth. The old Pawnees were especially funny because it seemed they were running in place with arms thrashing and all the body parts moving but the feet unable to keep up with the mind's will to escape the peril. The Welshman who is generally the reticent type was laughing so hard and uncontrollably that he pissed his pants. Some of the lads were not shy about giving him a dose of his own medicine by asking if, "Do you need your Mum to change your knickers?" and "Hey Griffith, youse supposed to pull it out of your breeches afore ya' start to piss," and "It ain't Saturday and time for a bath yet Griffith so whyse ya' all wet?" This teasing put the Welshman back in his usual humor as he hurried off to change his pants.

When the Indians figured out that locomotive wasn't going to hurt them, they all came back and took a second gander at it.
JM

Summer Nebraska Storm

The days of late have been miserable with the heat and sun bearing down on us something terrible. It takes the energy right out of a man and he can barely pull up his hammer to strike the spike and the shovel seems to be limp in his hands. That is until today.

A slow wind began blowing over us, gently sweeping away the sweat on our brows and neck and providing a bit of refreshment. I hardly noticed but was glad for the relief. Soon, I thought I heard the low rumble of cannon fire like that I was used to hearing in the war. Me and the other lads took notice of that straight away and looked off to the horizon and saw flat gray clouds forming over the prairie and heading our way. A wall of gray rain appeared to cover one end of the prairie and was moving sideway toward our direction. Flashes of lightning arced back and forth across the sky but no report of thunder came for a long time after.

The men were glad at the sight but didn't say anything. They kept swinging the hammer and shoveling the dirt but we knew the work day would be shortened and somehow were restored from our lethargy due to the heat.

As the wind began to gust, the grass started swirling and rustling, laying over a bit, picking up trails of dust and hurling them in confused circles around the wagons. The temperature dropped a few degrees straight away. Young mules started to bray and the horses snorted and whinnied in protest at the approaching storm. Canvas on the tents fluttered at a steady rhythm flapping and slapping at the openings and pushing over the ropes that held them in place. Men stood upright to catch the breeze full against their bodies as the sweat of the day was swept clean away.

The walking boss shouted "Put the tools away, that's it 'til she's passed," was met with hollers of approval. Immediately the clang of steel on steel ceased, replaced with only the crunching of loose dirt and gravel underneath the soles of the men's feet as they moved away from the grade. Wagons and teams turned their rigs away with the clanking of chains and rusty springs squeaking at the rise and fall of the wheels turning over the berms.

No sooner had we walked away from the work site did someone shout, "Look over there!" A blackish funnel started curving down out of the clouds very slowly, just a wisp at first and started to grow in size and breadth. Hail began to fall and men and livestock started to show signs of panic at the falling balls of ice. Cracks of the thunder sounded like cannon fire on the battlefield with vicious roars that could be felt through a man. Our gangs ran for cover underneath the wagons and railroad cars to escape the pelting they were getting from the sky. One mule was not so lucky, getting knocked off his feet by a ball of ice that was the size of a man's fist. Horses reared and kicked against their harnesses turning over wagons and running off in a panic dragging gear behind them. It was no use chasing them because to do so might get you knocked out like that unlucky mule.

The cloud was now touching the ground and nothing but a wall of black could be seen in front. It twisted back and forth over the ground, pulling up grass and dirt and the debris circled this monster in slow upward sweeping arcs into the sky. The noise was deafening as I watched this thing move over the prairie with the hail pounding the ground, the crack of thunder and the shriek of the wind in my ears. I lay under a car safe from the beating outside but unable to move away from the horrible sight in front of my eyes. I had heard of these things but had never seen one and I have to say I was in awe of the immense size of the tornado.

Very shortly, the storm began to ease. The cloud re-emerged into the black base from whence it came and was seen no more. The hail ceased and was replaced with rain and poured on us steady for the rest of the day leaving big muddy patches in camp, collapsed tents, wagons and tools flung over the landscape from the panic created earlier by the now passive rain clouds.

When this passes, it will be very busy time with General Jack urging us to lay even more track each day and catch up for the time we lost. Until then, I am going to enjoy the cool winds brought by this summer rain.

JM

Julesburg, Colorado 1867

General Jack came into camp today along with Mr. Dan looking for volunteers to clear out some claim jumping gamblers that have set their sights on railroad land in the town of Julesburg, Colorado. Me and Quinn said we would help out if we were needed and several other men off our crew said they would help also.

General Dodge it seems gave those fellows an ultimatum; to give up the land they was squatting on or get removed by force. Seeing how General Dodge and General Jack was both in the war during the rebellion, I would take them at their word. But gamblers and pimps ain't all that smart it seems and they will run a bluff as long as possible until it is clear you mean business. I reckon once they see us going in armed, they won't want to tangle with us but you never know.

I don't know why anybody would want to fight for that piece of land anyhow. This is one of the most barren, windswept, deserted places that has no attraction to any normal person at all. Granted the town is just a stone's throw away from the South Platte and it used to be a jumping off point for the Pony Express but with the railroad coming in here, all that don't mean a hill of buffalo chips.

Well, if them fellows want a fight, I am glad to oblige them. That band of riff raff has cheated, stolen and murdered many a man off this crew and like the saying goes, "What goes around, comes around." Many fellows on our crews were soldiers during the rebellion on both sides and I reckon almost every man knows how to shoot a gun. I don't like the idea of getting shot by that scum but I don't like them telling us what they are and ain't going to do neither.

JM

The Deadline Passes - Julesburg, Colorado 1867

General Jack and Mr. Dan called us men together today to let us know that those gamblers haven't cleared off the squatted on land like they was supposed to do. "We are going to forcibly remove them," said General Jack. Mr. Dan got the gunsmith to pass out rifles to those of who volunteered so that we can go into Julesburg as a show of force.

We marched into Julesburg from our camp and some of the more boastful of the gamblers were out in the street to meet us. They had a lot of swagger and some were drinking but they didn't show any fear or respect of General Jack. Others just went about their business like they were not concerned at what we might do. More came out to the street to watch what they thought was a Shakespearean play unfold with the opening of the Act I curtain rising for their enjoyment.

To his credit, General Jack did not respond at all to their ridicule about his size or his mission but simply read the directive from the company ordering their immediate removal from the lands allotted to the Union Pacific Railway. He held the declaration in one hand and his bullwhip in the other and his nerves and voice were as steady as could be. After he finished reading, he shouted to everyone in the streets that those who do not wish to be apart of this confrontation have two minutes to disperse. He took out his pocket watch and began looking at the dials from time to time and as well as around the street for someone who might take a pot shot at him.

I started getting scared. My hands were starting to sweat and my knees felt like they were knocking together. My breathing got heavier and heavier and my throat dried up. I have never fired on anybody, even during the war though I seen it done more times than I care to remember. Those two minutes seemed like an eternity and I stood there holding my rifle in my hand hoping nobody would see me trembling. Why didn't those gamblers just give up and move off like they was supposed to?

Soon enough, General Jack turned to us and said in a subdued voice, "Open fire, men. Use any means necessary to remove these squatters."

Those buffoons were still carrying on and laughing when General Jack gave the order. Things seemed to be moving twice as slow as normal after that. The men from our side of the line lowered their rifles at the mob of gamblers and drunkards jeering us in the street. General Jack leveled his pistol at them as well. When they realized what was happening and it was not a bluff, they reached and pulled up their sidearms and began to aim in our direction. A thunderclap of exploding powder shattered my ears as scores of bullets flew from our guns toward the rabble in the street. The slaps of the projectiles hitting the flesh followed by the crumpling bodies falling to the ground was the first report we were in a for real shooting fight. A black powdery veil lifted from the guns and began to obscure our view of the street.

I knew better from the war to stand still in one place when someone is shooting at you so I moved away from the crowd and started toward the mob down the side of the street. I lifted my gun and aimed toward the middle of all those moving and shooting bodies and luckily, I didn't seem to draw the attention of anyone. I fired my gun and started shooting as quickly as I could. Each time I fired off a round, I saw someone in the mob drop down out of sight so hopefully I was hitting what I aimed for.

One of our fellows took a kerosene lamp that was lit and threw it into one of those gambling houses. It lit up in no time at all spreading to the floor and walls. Others from our crew came and tore down the makeshift buildings and tents, using their rifle butts, horses and lassoes and so forth to pull them down.

Before long, it was total chaos. Horses were bucking and kicking to get away from the noise and carnage. People were running in all directions shooting at anything. Black powder smoke filled the street and it was hard to breathe and even harder to see with that cloud hovering over the melee. Men on both sides were cursing the other, wounded were calling out to their friends for help. Some of those gamblers stood fast in the street trying to re-load their pistols while our men drew down a bead on them and shot them where they stood, leaving them in a heap on the muddy street.

The gamblers started backing away slowly down the street and General Jack urged the men forward. Our men kept firing at a steady pace now with their pistols and rifles leaving more and more bodies in the street as we advanced. Hardly any of our men were getting hit as we kept the pressure on. Soon, those gamblers that were left turned tail and ran away after they looked around them and saw that hardly any of their companions were standing.

When they were all gone, General Jack told us to burn all the squatters buildings and tents which we did right away. It was big old bon fire to be sure and the flames of that torching reminded some of those fellows of General Sherman's march through Georgia according to those men who were there during the rebellion.

General Jack called us together after we had finished and congratulated us on a good job well done. He promised us a bonus for bravery and an extra ration of tobacco for which the men cheered when they heard that. Soon the wagons were coming in and we were gathering those of ours who had been wounded or killed and thankfully there weren't many. On the other hand, we were going to have to dig a lot of graves for all the gamblers that were killed. I don't rightly know how many for sure met their maker that day because the accounts get more exaggerated each time someone tells the story.

I was tired all right from that but mainly from all the excitement. I reckon those gamblers had it coming but I didn't feel good about what had happened. I don't like killing and I reckon anyone that does has something wrong with him. Father Costigan told me once that there is evil in the world and the only way to stop evil is by superior force. "Good doesn't always win the day," he told me as a lad, "but it is up to us to see that we do our best that it does." Those gamblers were stealing and many of them would kill you for what you have in your pocket. Stealing to my way of thinking is one step away from murder. If someone is willing to take away your ability to earn money in an honest way like those gamblers, they would have no problem seeing you starve after they have all that you own neither. They were warned and they made the wrong choice. The consequences are theirs.

August 1867 Sidney, Nebraska

We have terrible news today that has put every man on edge. The Cheyenne have derailed a train, attacked a work crew and slaughtered all the men except one. A fellow by the name of Thompson survived but it would have almost been better for him if he didn't.

When he realized what was going on after the train jumped the track, he commenced to running but one of the Cheyenne warriors caught up with him on the horseback and hit him over the head with a rifle butt. Thompson laid down and pretended he was dead and that brave stood over him and started sawing away at his scalp. He said the pain was so intense he could barely stand it but he thought it better to do that than fight back and guarantee his death.

He laid there almost two hours before he got up the courage to move and by this time the Cheyenne had moved off. He started running down the track, holding his scalp in a bucket and soon enough caught up with another train and flagged it down. That train was heading directly into the wreck behind him and it was good that he caught them or they would have derailed as well.

Thompson saved that train and that crew but it is not for sure whether he is going to make it or not. He brought his scalp back in a bucket of water hoping someone could sew it back on but it ain't likely. One of the fellows that looked at it said it looked like a drowned rat, a horrible sight. I hope the doctor can save Mr. Thompson.

The lads' reactions are what you might expect under the circumstances ranging from intense fear to overwhelming anger and grief. One Irish fellow who had friends on the crew cried just like a newborn babe without the least bit of shame for his lost friends. One or two had families back East; now they are orphaned and widowed. Mr. Casement has given permission to hold a wake for the men in honor of their memory.

Some of the gang went to Sgt. O'Halloran demanding to know what he and his men will do to avenge the crew, to protect us from attacks and so forth. Some simply said they had enough of this and will return East on the first available train.

Most of the men who fought in the war, both from the North and South have decided to stay on because they consider the risk from the Indians much less than fighting that went on recently. I count myself among those that wish to remain for a number of reasons, the least of which there is no work and no home to return to in Philadelphia. General Dodge we are told has sent a request to General Sherman making sure we are better protected but in the meantime has made sure that rifles are available to us on the work crews. Those who have no experience with guns were given lessons on the fundamentals of shooting a gun, how to take aim, lead your target and squeeze the trigger by the some of the cavalry sergeants. I would not count myself a marksman so I took the opportunity to make sure my aim was steady and true as before. I didn't carry more than a pistol during the war as driving cattle was not nearly as dangerous as hiding behind a split rail fence shooting across an open field or crouching against an earthen mound while cannon fire plowed the ground up beneath a body. Luckily my hand and my vision are still good and I was able to hit my target successfully from 100 yards away.

The intensity of the men's rage was clear when they came in from the evening after making the rounds at the saloons, swearing every curse and oath toward the red man. Some said they would scalp the first redskin they come across, whether they were Cheyenne, Sioux or Pawnee, it didn't matter. The only sensible solution was to clear them all out from the nation so a white man could traverse the country without fear of losing his life and even worse, his scalp to the uncivilized peoples who occupied this country. I understand their anger but this type of talk is all nonsense. I didn't say a word in response but I don't agree. Better to let the loudmouths blather on and get a decent night sleep than to argue with the fools and be drawn into a fight that will profit a man nothing.

JM

Attack on the Pawnee squaw

Tonight I woke up to the sound of a woman screaming like a banshee and shouting gibberish I couldn't understand. I thought I was dreaming at first but then I heard it mixed in with some curses men use around here and I knew I wasn't. I hurried to put on my trousers and boots and went running toward the sound of the noise. There in the shadows I saw three men dragging a woman by the hair with her kicking and putting up a fight, giving a good account for her self, swinging her fists at the air and not really connecting. One of the men hit her in the face with his fist like he would a man which infuriated me.

When I got up close I could see it was that Pawnee woman that Sgt. O'Halloran brought in from the plains that had been held by the Sioux. She was still spewing out curses in her own language at these men and I saw that her clothes had been ripped from the struggle.

"What's all this?" says I. "What are you doing to this woman the three of you?"

"Mind your own business, McGlinchey," was the reply of one of the men. I knew from the sound of his voice it was that Jack Foley fellow who was all the time lending money to the men for drink at usury. He was a small, mean man whose heart was black as Satan's and don't think twice about breaking a fellow's hands with a maul if he don't have the money to pay. The other two I didn't know but they were big fellas and looked to Jack for some re-assurance about what they was doing now that the three of them was caught in the act of their vile intent.

"You'll be letting that woman go," says I. "She obviously don't want nothing to do with the lot of ya'.

"I done told you to mind your own business and I won't be telling you again," says Foley. "Them redskins don't have no problem with murdering and raping our white women... scalping our boys on the work gangs...so we intend to repay them, that's all," he said with a drunken slur.

"You'll not be doing any such thing, least ways not with this woman who had nothing do with that. She was a prisoner of the Sioux and probably has her own grievances against them," says I.

"She's a redskin, ain't she? One's the same as the others far as we are concerned," says one of Foley's thugs. "Hold her Will," he says to his companion, "while I take care of this jackass who can't mind his own business."

No sooner had Will pinned her arms behind her back did the other come at me swinging and throwing wild punches at me. I side stepped him quite easily and gave him a punch to the stomach that doubled him over. Foley came in right behind him hitting me on the back of my head with something that made my vision kind of blurry but he didn't connect cleanly or otherwise I would be knocked cold. The other came rushing me but again I sidestepped him and was looking around for Foley when I see two forms emerge from the shadows carrying pick handles.

I heard a 'swoosh' through the air as the swing of the handle came rushing toward the one trying to fight with me. A crack of wood splitting against the man's skull resonated in the otherwise still night and saw that Hoppin' John has knocked the man off of his feet and the impact of the blow had carried him another 10 feet landing on his back. The man lay motionless on the prairie as I looked for sign of Foley who was getting up to make a run for it. No sooner had Hoppin' John laid the one fighting me out did I hear the sound of another 'swoosh and crack' against the head of the fellow named Will, the one had the Pawnee woman's arms pinned behind her. He crumpled over in a ball on top of the squaw and there behind him was Quinn looking mighty angry at this sight.

By this time, Foley could see the fight was lost. He began to run and got about 15 yards away when Quinn threw his pick handle at him and knocked his legs out from under him. Collapsing on the ground, I could see Foley searching for something inside of his coat as the three of us began walking toward him. Quinn got there first and kicked at his hand thrust inside his jacket, throwing a small derringer a few yards away and landing on the ground. Hoppin' John walked to the other side and stood on his other hand pinning him to the ground.

Quinn didn't say nothing to Foley. He stood on his other free hand and stared at him like he was about to kill him. He stared at him a good 20 seconds and then reached into his pocket and pulled out a knife. "So you like to rape women, do you?" says Quinn. Before I could say a word, he had bent over and cut a big one inch square notch in the top of Foley's ear leaving Foley screaming and cursing. "Now the women you meet will know what kind of man you are," says Quinn. "Let him up, Hoppin' John."

As we turned to walk away, we heard Foley groaning and cursing. "This ain't over Quinn. I'll get the three of you if takes the rest of my days. I'LL KILL ALL YOU SONS OF BITCHES."

I took the Pawnee woman with me and was going to guard her out on the prairie that night nearby so no other harm might come to her. The next day, I would make sure Sgt. O'Halloran got her back to her own people as soon as he could. This woman's life wouldn't be worth a plug nickel as long as Foley and his type were around and a friend of his might try getting at us by hurting her. Regardless, the three of us would have to sleep with one eye open from now on or hope that Foley and his group would be afraid of us now. Cowards like Foley are opportunists and I think we had better keep our guard up, just the same.

JM

The Day After

Word of what happened last night has spread through the camp like wildfire. Men who gave no regard to Quinn at all now look at him with a little more scrutiny out of the corner of their eye. Even Hoppin' John is enjoying his new status as the men seem to accept him a little more than they did before.

I haven't seen those other two that were with Foley but you can be sure they are lurking around here somewhere nursing their wounds and waiting for the right opportunity to stick a knife in one or all our backs.

Most of the men have come down on our side of the issue even though they give no account for a squaw. She is a human being and it don't hold no water with them to take out revenge on an innocent for those who done the scalping and murdering of our men. Soldiers on both sides didn't tolerate that sort of thing back during the war and I don't think nothing has changed to make it different for a Pawnee squaw.

McIlheny, one of the men on the Foley's grading crew told me that Foley is staying at the infirmary with the doctor while his ear heals. He went in there telling him he got jumped at shantytown but I don't think the doctor cares what story he brings to him or what happened to him. He has heard all the lies that a man could hear about this and that and he patched him up the best he could. He got a bit of a fever and will probably be unable to work for a few days until he gets over it.

Several times, General Jack gave me long looks today and I ain't quite sure if it had anything to do with the goings on but he didn't say nothing which is fine by me. I don't want to call no attention to myself and the sooner this thing passes, the better.

Sgt. O'Halloran took that Pawnee woman off to her own people today and he promised me he would look after her until he could get her situated with another of her own kind. The Sergeant is a fine man who is a good example not only to his men but to anyone who comes in contact with him. I wished we had more men out here on the frontier like him and I can promise you we could do with his type. His men think the world of him and the Lieutenant considers every word the same as that uttered by one of the Apostles.

It's funny, that woman didn't say nothing to me or anyone else when they was getting ready to leave. Course, she don't know hardly any English either but she just looked at me with sort of a blank stare and rode off with the Sergeant and a couple of Pawnee scouts. I smiled and waved at her as she went away and she just lifted her hand in a mechanical way.

I guess after all she been through, escaping from the Sioux, walking around the prairie all hungry and just barely alive, getting rescued only to get nearly raped by bunch of savage white men it would pretty much shake up anybody. She got the same look that some of the Southerners had after the Union Army came through burning their towns. They knew their world wasn't ever going to be the same and the expression on their faces said it all. Women in the South would break down and start crying sometimes when all they had was destroyed and especially if they lost a loved one but I don't think that is the way Indian women carry on.

She is like one of those Greek Stoics Father Costigan talked about when James and I were in school in Philadelphia. He said they wouldn't do anything to give away any emotions and I kind of find that hard to believe. How can someone not have any emotions? Still, this Pawnee woman didn't show any and I hope she will be fine. I will make sure to ask Sgt. O'Halloran how she fared when he returns.

A Mormon Family Heads West

Today a group of Mormons came near the camp getting their wagon train prepared for the long journey out to the Utah territory. They normally go off in bunches of 50 wagons or so escorted by the Army but this one was a little bit short of that number but never did you see such a close group of people in such a small outfit. It seems they were all related somehow or another and I don't mean kissing cousins.

The leader of the group had himself seven wives, all different ages and looks. He wasn't much of a man to look at, short and stout physically but you could tell by the way he carried himself he had the respect of the people that were with him. I had a chance to speak with him briefly but I didn't get into the details of his religion or why he had all those wives and kids and such. I could see the advantages of all that but the Catholic Church has come down dead set against such a thing because it would hurt the family. If they are so concerned about the family, they should consider making drinking a mortal sin so the Irish fathers would look after their children half as good as these Mormons do. But that's another story.

Anyway, I got to talking to one of his daughters whose name was Patience. Her name fit her very well because she was a young lady who carried herself with a demeanor that was respectful toward everyone she came in contact; all the wives her father had, all the bothers and sisters, half brothers and sisters, cousins and even the soldiers and workers who leered at her from time to time cause they ain't seen many white women out here that has all their teeth or ain't a whore or some such thing. Patience is 15 years old right now and she was out gathering buffalo chips to put in a blanket suspended under the wagon for fuel to cook with. I knew where there was a good patch of chips not far off and I invited her and some of her sisters to come along and I would show them where to find it.

I whistled for Colleen to come along and she jumped up from her spot in the shade, happy to go for a walk out on the prairie. She ran on ahead of us looking over this patch of grass or that, trying to scare up a rabbit for her to chase so she could impress us.

Patience and I began to talking about all sorts of things, how they got here from Illinois, what they were going to do in Utah. I told her I came out here after the war and she said that it was a terrible thing and many people she knew back in Illinois had been injured horribly from battlefield wounds, some losing their legs and arms from the balls festering inside their bodies so they had to be amputated and all. She said she hoped she could learn how to take care of sick people and maybe when she got to Utah, she would find someone who could teach her. She already knew a lot about midwifery from all the brothers, sisters, half brothers and half sisters, cousins and such she helped deliver.

"That's a good start," I said.

She told me her father was probably going to marry her off within the next year once they got to Utah. Said she hoped it wasn't to a really old man and already asked her father to please not give her away to some old codger. One girlfriend of hers that wasn't traveling with them was almost 17 when she married off to a man almost 40. The man already had two other wives and she didn't like it much but that was her lot in life to be a good wife and mother.

I didn't know what to say to her. Under different circumstances, I think Patience would make a fine wife for just about anybody but I couldn't imagine her being the wife of a man who had several other wives or married to a 40-year-old man either. On the other hand, I couldn't see me doing them Mormon things neither just for a young woman like Patience. They are a tight knit group with some funny ideas but I enjoyed her company nonetheless and we had a fine time gathering the chips, laughing and making jokes.

She pelted me with one of the dry chips when my back was turned and pretended she didn't do it, looking the other way when I turned around. I started walking toward her slowly and she looked at me out the corner of her eye and gave a scream and started running, throwing the chips from her apron and giving a good account of herself considering she was in a dress. Colleen

Irish Gandy Dancer

started running after the two us barking and wagging her tail trying to figure out what all the commotion was about. I caught up with her and grabbed her by the arm and she squealed and laughed and half heartedly demanded I let her go. I did but I had the urge to kiss her which I didn't. I think she would have let me but there were too many people around and I wouldn't want to embarrass her or me.

We re-gathered the chips and started back toward their camp talking and speculating what the trip out west had in store for us. I was going with the work gang and she with her band of Mormon brothers, sisters, cousins and every relative in between with the Army along to guard them. They leave in a few days and maybe I will drop by to say farewell before they go into the wilderness.

JM

Mr. Dan calls me in

Today was a bad day because I had to clear my name in front of Mr. Dan Casement on account of some fellow accusing me of stealing. Not that we have any shortage of thieves around these parts but I ain't one of 'em and any man that calls me one had best be ready to defend himself.

Anyway, I was out preparing the grade with some of the other fellows on the gang when the foreman comes over and says that Mr. Dan wants me to come see him right away. I asked him where Mr. Dan was at the moment and he said in a tent about a mile back down the track. So, I starts walking that way wondering all the while what is it he wants with the likes of me. I ain't no one of account and I search my mind with no answer coming to me.

As I get to Mr. Dan's tent, I announce myself and take off me hat as Mr. Dan invites me in. Mr. Dan is a short man but not a person to be trifled with. He is stout as a tree stump and he is standing behind a makeshift desk looking me over. I am still curious as to what this is all about and he says to me, "McGlinchey, I have heard a report that you have been stealing not only from the company but from the men. A thief in an outfit can bring down the spirits of the men in no time at all and I won't stand for it. Worse yet, we can not tolerate someone stealing from the company. Unless you can refute these charges, I am afraid I will have to dismiss you."

I stood there stunned and you could have knocked me over with a feather. I think my mouth was open a full five seconds before I got my wits about me and an anger started growing within me that I could barely hold back.

Even though I was angry, I said in a very controlled voice, "Not a word of this is true, Sir. Mr. Dan, who is accusing me of these horrible things? I would like to question my accuser if I may."

"I agree, McGlinchey. I don't believe any man should be found guilty on the testimony of one man and therefore, I will do just that," Mr. Dan responded. "Tell Berkely to come to my tent straight away," he told an assistant through the tent flap. Soon I heard the sound of footsteps fading away followed shortly by a pair of footsteps coming the direction of the tent entrance.

An enormous man ducked down to enter through the opening of the tent and could barely stand upright as he erected himself in front of Mr. Dan. This man was well over 6 feet tall and then some and I didn't recall where I knew him from, if at all. How could this man I didn't know be accusing me of stealing?

"Tell me what you told me before Berkely," directed Mr. Dan.

"It's as I told you before Sir, I seen this fellow going through the men's personal belongings when they were not around and supposed to be at their work. He took some money and other things from several bunks that were not his and hid them away," Berkely replied.

"That's a bloody lie," says I. "I never seen you before and I don't know what your game is but you will retract that mendacity of yours."

"You are a theefffff...." Berkely couldn't get the word out cause I could no longer able to control my temper. I brought my boot up off of the floor and came down solid on top of this giant's kneecap, buckling his leg and sending him sprawling to the floor.

I took hold of Berkely's hand and twisted in a downward motion where any movement he made, any pressure I applied and he would be in excruciating pain. I gave him a twist just to let him know I was in charge to which he let out a yell of a banshee.

71

"Who put you up to this lie?" says I, giving him a twist on the hand. "Tell me or I will do this to you all day."

"Go piss yourself," says Berkely. "I ain't telling you nuttin'."

I gave Berkely another twist and I could feel the tendons moving in his arm stretching to the breaking point. "Who put you up to this?" I demanded.

"Stop, you are breaking my arm," says Berkely. "All right, let go. It was Foley. He said he would pay me $20 to say you were stealing from the men."

"Are you goin' to behave if I let you up?" says I.

"Let him up," said Mr. Dan who now had a pistol drawn on the man. I let the fellow go but he didn't bother to move but just lay there. He slowly dragged himself up and saw Mr. Dan's pistol aimed at him and just looked downward at the floor, knowing what was coming.

"Get out of this camp," said Mr. Dan. "If I see you here again, I will have you bullwhipped or shot if you resist."

The man turned to walk out but didn't bother to look either of us in the eye.

Mr. Dan turned to me as he put the pistol back in his holster and said, "My apologies McGlinchey. I am responsible to the men on this crew and the Union Pacific and have to investigate these types of things. Sadly, it turns out it was someone who was trying to slander your name."

"Yes, sir," says I. "No harm done and I appreciate you giving me the chance to clear me self."

I won't make the same mistake again. Do you want me to take care of the Foley fellow or would you rather do it yourself?" asked Mr. Dan.

"If you don't mind, sir, I will take care of it myself," says I.

"I thought you would say that," Mr. Dan answered. "A very unfortunate business McGlinchey, very unfortunate indeed. You may return to your duties."

"Yes, sir," I replied. I walked out of the tent thinking where I would find that wretch of a creature Foley. I knew that Berkely would head straight for him. It didn't matter because as soon as he found out, he would surround himself with more of his thugs and I would have little chance to get at him, even if I brought me own gun. Last I heard, he was 60 miles up the track digging new grades with his crew and it wasn't likely I could take the time off to get to him anyhow.

I knew he wouldn't stop now that he couldn't get me fired. I would have to sleep with one eye open for sure because the next time would probably mean a knife or gunshot in my back if I knew his type.

JM

Wyoming - November, 1867

There has been some grumbling among the men about our wages as of late. There are hardly two dimes to rub together between all the work gangs. The men have been without pay for several months and with no sight of the paymaster's car coming over the horizon. Rumors are filling the air that the whole project is to be abandoned and the men dispersed. I personally don't believe that. My experience during the rebellion reminds me the speed that a rumor can circulate and the more outrageous the lie, the quicker it is to be believed by the simple minded folk.

Some of the men have been buying drinks on credit or borrowing money at usury and the saloon keepers are starting to demand that accounts be settled. The fact they sell water-downed whiskey and tea to the dancing girls that give the men a bit of company is neither hear nor there when the barkeep tallies the evening's expenses. They want payment for their services the same as the men who dig the cuts, grade the roads and drive the spikes.

The Casement brothers thought the situation of our wages required it be addressed by them to allay any rumors of the Union Pacific defaulting on their obligations. In meetings held along the track, General Jack and his brother Dan would have the work gangs gathered round so they could speak to the men directly about the situation. These two brothers have fearsome reputations which I thought quite odd when I first saw them.

The brothers rode into our camp on the back of two very fine horses, one a bay mare and the other a chestnut gelding, several hands taller than an average horse. The quality of the horses did not go unnoticed by the men who looked on them with a bit of envy.

Mr. Dan Casement got down from his horse and walked over to a stack of railroad ties that lay nearby. Even with his hat, Mr. Dan is hardly much over 5 feet tall and there was some lads that made no attempt to disguise their humor at the sight of such a short man. Dan turned to look over at them, his face revealing little about his mood, and said nothing about the slight as he motioned to the men to gather round so he could speak to them.

Mr. Dan started off telling us who he was for those who didn't know and began speaking to us about the situation, assuring us that wages would be coming soon and to not fret about it. He went on to say he understood our frustration and would work as quickly as possible to get the wages owed us even if meant he would pay us out of his own pocket. I thought him a sincere man since our first meeting and one whose word could be trusted. Some of the lads off to the right of the assembly started to grumble aloud and showing signs of their disapproval. One of them, a large man who laughed at Mr. Dan when he dismounted his horse, stepped forward and called Mr. Dan a liar to his face. He stood easily over 6 feet tall and had a barrel for a chest and began poking Dan in the chest and telling him in a drunken slur that he would have his wages now.

Mr. Dan's face turned mighty dark at man calling him a liar. He grasped the finger of the man and turned his wrist over in a quick motion and the drunken Irishman soon was on the ground yelling in agony. One his friends stepped forward to pull Mr. Dan off of him but General Jack had his bullwhip off his saddle horn in no time at all and the crack of the leather could be heard as the cord wrapped around the other man's foot. General Jack pulled the man off his feet with one pull and soon gave him another crack of the whip to cut the tip of nose to remind him of his station.

General Jack shouted aloud, "Will there be any other questions men?" to which none of the men replied. General Jack told his brother Dan to let the man up. As the two arose, the General told them their services were no longer required and asked the men assembled if there were others who would like to join them. None stepped forward. They bid their farewells to the foreman and rode off to speak to the next work gang further on up the track.

JM

Rose comes for her man

One of the biggest women I ever saw today came down to the work site. A fella on my gang named Eamon says to me she is a laundress who works over in the shantytown. She was easily over six feet tall and wide across the shoulders as any man who works on our gangs. She had forearms like those men who worked the docks back in South Philadelphia and a severe look about her. You couldn't help but notice her as she walked toward our crew with her head uncovered and a squalling baby in her arms. I reckon no bonnet in the West was big enough to cover that mess of bright red hair. She walked up to the foreman and seemed to have a bit polite conversation with him and he pointed in a direction and off she went.

Soon she was behind a small man who was shoveling the dirt near a grade and without missing a beat, knocked his derby off of him and shouted, "Don't pretend you don't know I'm behind you Mr. Thomas Kiernan."

Turning with a bit of surprise in his face, he says to her, "Rose, my dear, is that you who has come to visit me?"

"I'll have none of your nonsense Mr. Kiernan," says she staring down at his five foot frame. "You know what I am here for and you'll be doing the right thing by me and your baby."

"Of course my dear, of course. But we have no preacher here so as soon as one arrives, we can tie the knot and be wed."

"Is that so?" says she. "The last time you had to get the blessing of your parents. Then one of your friends tells me your mum and dad is dead. The time before that, you wanted to buy me a dress for the occasion but you lost your money at cards. Well, I got good news for you Mr. Kiernan. A preacher just rode into camp today and says he will marry us straight away."

Kiernan's face went pale at the news and Rose wasted no time thrusting that massive arm toward his ear and pulling him off his feet. "Stand up you daft fool," say she. "And get your hat."

Scooping up his hat, Kiernan and Rose strode toward the shanties with him struggling to keep up and she held a firm grip on his ear. Protesting and negotiating, Kiernan did his best to stay up but kept slipping on the loose dirt but Rose's grip was firm and didn't allow him to slip away.

No man on the crew had a dry eye that day for laughing so hard at the sight of those two walking away. Rose kept her dignity throughout the ordeal while Kiernan begged for her to release her grip on him. The foreman shouted after him, "You can have the day off to celebrate the blessed event of your wedding Kiernan," to which every man laughed all the harder at the doomed expression on his face.

JM

Buffalo Hunters

Today Quinn and I went to the end of the track and took the wagon to where the grading gang was working the new site. I don't know why I was asked instead of told to come along except maybe Mr. Dan figures the men will listen to me if I have something to say and he wanted me to have a look at the area. It was good enough that I was not swinging a hammer or pick today but it sure enough was hot enough to cook an egg on the rocks around us.

Shimmering waves rose up out of the prairie as the mules plodded along over the rough patches of land along side the grade our gangs were building. Brown patches of dry grass were waiting for a bit of rain to turn them green again but the sky showed no sign of relenting. The grades were not near ready to go as I looked back over the emerging mounds piling up for us to lay track over.

The wagon rocked back and forth as we plodded along and I almost could have fallen asleep to the swaying if it weren't for the heat. My clothes were drenched with sweat and I had to lift my hat up off my brow many times to wipe the moisture away that was pouring down into my eyes, stinging them to tears.

Before long, a smell like that I remember crossing over the battlefields in the South caught my nose. The smell of rotting flesh, a smell so foul that no person who ever has come across it will likely put it out of their mind any time soon. I turned to look over my shoulder to where the smell was coming from and saw off in the distance the shape of mounds that rose ever so slightly off the prairie. Buzzards were circling overhead, swirling and swooping down onto the area where all the mounds were.

"What's that over there?" says I to no one in particular.

"Buffalo," said the teamster who was driving us.

There before us, scattered over the ground, were hundreds of buffalo carcasses lying in the sun. There innards were starting to swell up and the gas they were putting off was something terrible. When the buzzards began picking away at their innards, the gas gave off a stench that hovered and with the sun as hot as it was, it cooked their innards ever so slowly making the smell that much harder to tolerate.

I got out my kerchief and wrapped it around my head but it did little to relieve me of the dreadful smell.

Buffalo hunters came through here a few days earlier and was clearing out a large herd here so they don't get in the way of the train or knock over the telegraph poles as they are inclined to do when they feel like scratching their neck or head, which is pretty much all the time with all the fleas they are carrying. Even more to the point, killing the buffalo will make it pretty hard for Red Cloud and the Sioux to eat and I think that is pretty much what General Sherman has in mind, to make life so difficult for the red man they will have to stop killing the white man and live on the reservations.

It's a sad thing for the Indians but their way of life is over. General Sherman will fight them the same way he fought the Southerners during the rebellion and that is to take away

80

everything they got to fight back with and burn their teepees down around them. Sooner or later, they are going to get hungry and will have to submit or die. Some of the young braves I hear swore they will not stop fighting no matter what but some of the elders of the Sioux tribes see no way out of the white man's progress.

We passed through the field of carcasses, seeing buzzards hop from one animal to another. It was an amazing sight but not nearly so much as the one we were about to see. About five minutes driving into the field of carcasses, the wagon stopped and we came up alongside a corpse that had been mutilated something horrible. Arrows had pierced every part of the body which now was a mat of dried blood and cut up parts. The man's legs were sawed in two at the knees and the muscles, what was left of them sliced like a butcher might. He had his eyes gouged out and his ears were cut off. I recognized the clothes this was man had strewn about him. He wore a bright red shirt that was now in shreds along with some very small shoes.

It was Foley, the man who swore to kill me. I heard he got in over his head with some of the hard cases in the shantytown and had to make tracks 'cause he got in a shooting argument.

I heard the argument was over a whore but it really doesn't matter since he killed a man for no good reason and had to run for his life. He disappeared that night after stealing a horse and I guess he got lost because he started heading off in the wrong direction. Apparently the Sioux found him in the field of freshly killed buffalo and decided to take their anger out on him. Lord, even though he was no good, I would hate to have witnessed the fury of that revenge they took out on him.

Me and Quinn took our shovels and began to digging. There was no point in trying to gather up what was left of Foley because his parts was spread all over the prairie, in part by the wild animals and in part by the Indians. We scooped up the parts as best we could and tossed them into a hole, deep enough for the animals not to be digging him up hopefully. Even though I am sure he is in the infernal reaches with all the sin he committed in this world, I said the Lord's Prayer over him just the same with Quinn holding his hat in his hand.

After that, we got in the wagon and headed back to our camp but nobody said a thing.

JM

Gettysburg

I am in Gettysburg. The day is bright and with the sun reflecting on the corn stalks in the fields around. There is a sense of peace in the air but the feeling seems wrong. "Is this Gettysburg?" I ask myself. It looks like it.

I see a man with no eyes standing motionless in front of me wearing tattered blue clothes and an arm missing from his body. He says nothing to me but points the way with his other arm. I say nothing in return but follow the direction he is pointing. I pull the reins of my mount toward that direction and see a road in front of me. I am alone on the road and my horse and I move at an easy walk.

"Where is everybody else?" I am thinking. "Where are the other lads from the 116th"?

As I move down the lane, blood-stained grass mats the sides of the road but there are no bodies. The sun continues to shine and the day is fine. The birds sing and flit from branch to branch.

I ride ever so slowly another quarter of a mile. Off to the side of the road I see an arm that has been blown off from cannon fire. On the other side of the road, a leg and the torso of a man that is wearing a grey uniform of the rebel. Turn upward toward the sun, the prone body of a Connecticut corporal whose face has been blown to bits from a Minnie-ball. Soon bodies of men begin to be strewn here and there, more as I move further down this country lane.

The pleasant fields, the green trees, singing birds and sunshine have gone. All around me is scorched earth with bodies of men who have been massacred, their entrails hanging out of their bodies, the buzzards and crows hopping from the corpses picking off the soft fleshy parts of the eyes and other parts torn open from the artillery fire. Splintered trees are uprooted and twisted in a tortured manner. I am the only living person, moving steadily across the battlefield's aftermath. The stench of the decaying bloating bodies is causing my stomach to churn. The sulfuric smell of gunpowder and burned grass adds to the mix to make the smell even more putrid.

One of the dismembered corpses turns toward me and waves for me to come near him.

"McGlinchey," he calls me by name. He persists and motions for me to come nearer but I dare not. "McGlinchey," he repeats. Soon another corpse to the other side of my horse stands and walks toward me calling me, "McGlinchey." The sun brightens and intensifies on my face.

"McGlinchey." One of them has grabbed my by my arm and is pulling me....

I awake and next to me is Quinn. "What are you going on about boy-oh? You were shouting all kind of nonsense in your sleep. From the sound of it, a banshee had you by the shirt tail and was dragging you down to the depths. Are you going to be all right?"

I am awake and feel my heart racing and my breath coming in gasps. It is just a dream I remind myself.

"Yeah, I reckon I will. I guess that trip out to the buffalo grounds brought back some memories that I wish hadn't come up," says I. "I will be fine," I repeat to reassure myself and to Quinn.

"All right then, get some sleep," and try not to be dreaming of things such as that but the gold of the little people at the end of the rainbow, the castle you will building yourself in Texas, having more concubines than Solomon himself and which member of the House of Lords you will have doing your gardening and acting as your footstool for your easy chair," joked Quinn.

"Aye, that I will," I said with a laugh. I turned over to sleep and rolled around for a bit before I was sound asleep with no memory of the dreams that came after.

JM

I Get Promoted

Today General Jack called me aside and said he wanted to talk with me. I thought maybe I had done something wrong and was a bit worried that I was going to be sacked or given a tongue lashing for something I was not aware.

General Jack started off with, "McGlinchey, I have been watching you these past several months and you have the stamina of a mule and you are a quick learner. Not only that, you are an honest man and the men respect you. As you know, we are in an almighty rush to lay as much track as possible. We need men like yourself to lead crews of tracklayers and I want to make you the lead man on a crew of your own. You can pick the men you want to work on your crew but don't go fishing in someone else's pond if you get my meaning. I don't want any quarrels between my crews. You will get a wage of three dollars per day and of course if you lay two or more miles of track per day, you and your crew get double wages along with the other crews. Think you can handle it?"

You could have knocked me over with a feather I was so taken aback. I repeated the words slowly to him, "You want ME to run a crew?"

"Yes, I do," he replied, "if you think you can handle it."

"Yes General Casement. I would be proud to."

"All right then," he said. "Start picking out your team and let me know if you need anything else to get going. We will start first thing the day after tomorrow."

I knew straight away who I would get. Quinn for sure if he didn't mind me being the boss and Hoppin' John. I knew the men I had on my crew wouldn't mind Hoppin' John being there because he was such a powerful man, a strong worker that could go all day from sun up to sun down and not slow down a whit or show any sign of fatigue. If they didn't want to work with a Darky, they could go find another place but I would treat the men on my crew fair and I would expect the same in return from them.

Most importantly, I would not bring on any of the men who were known to drink all night and try to make it through the following day. I had in mind to make some money not only for myself by getting those bonuses but for the men on my crew and I wasn't going to have any shiftless slackers there holding us up. There were some newcomers on the grading crew that stayed in camp a lot and didn't go out too much. I would talk with some of them this evening and ask around. I can't wait to tell Quinn and Hoppin' John the news. Hopefully they will go along. I know they will but I got to ask them first.

Me, the lead man of a crew! If that don't beat all. I sure hope I don't let the General down or the men on my gang.

JM

Directors of the Union Pacific commemorate construction to the 100th Meridian
(Courtesy of Library of Congress)

General Jack Casement posing next to the rolling dormitories. Notice the tents on top of the rail cars, the General's whip and Russian fur hat. The former General continued to run his operations as he did in the military.

(Courtesy Utah State Historic Society)

Dan Casement, Business Manager for the construction of the Union Pacific
Courtesy Utah State Historic Society

Irish track layers posing for a photo. The workers normally handled the rails with tongs rather than their hands. (Courtesy Utah State Historic Society)

Union Pacific Railroad construction workers gather before the paymaster's car and the camera.
(Courtesy Utah State Historic Society)

Pawnee Indians fought for pay against the Sioux, helping keep workers for the Union Pacific a bit safer while working on the rail line.
Courtesy Library of Congress

Pawnee squaws and children. Notice the backpack
like carrier for the baby.
Courtesy Library of Congress

Aftermath of the Gettysburg battlefield. Many railroad workers were Irish migrants who fought for both North and South and brought bitter mental images like this of lost comrades when they migrated west. (Courtesy Library of Congress)

A pioneer family heading west (Courtesy Utah State Historic Society)

Wagon train loaded with supplies for construction department moving down Echo Canyon, Utah. (Courtesy Utah State Historic Society)

Union Pacific tunnel boring - Winter 1868
Courtesy Utah State Historic Society

Sign directing engineers to slow to four mile per hour prior to crossing bridge. Some bridges like the Dale Creek were considered flimsy at best and caused a great deal of anxiety for those first across. (Courtesy Utah State Historic Society)

Trestles, Dale Creek. Notice the guy wires to strengthen the bridge. During the initial construction, the bridge swayed under heavy winds giving second thoughts to those who considered crossing. (Courtesy Utah State Historic Society)

Mormon surveyors move their equipment up a cliff during
the construction of the Union Pacific.
Courtesy Utah State Historic Society

Trestle building, Green River Wyoming
(Courtesy Utah State Historic Society)

Digging a cut at Wilhelmina Pass
Courtesy Utah State Historic Society

Fear of Irish and Chinese immigration was widespread due to the importation of foreign labor for the construction of the railroad. A one panel, three scene cartoon showing, in the first scene, an Irish man with the head of Uncle Sam in his mouth and a Chinese man with the feet of Uncle Sam in his mouth, in the second scene they consume Uncle Sam, and in the third the Chinese man consumes the Irish man; on the landscape in the distant background are many railroads.

(Courtesy Library of Congress)

Telling Stories

Quinn and I finally got us a tent so that we can sleep away from the rolling dormitories. We will have to go back in there during the winter time but for now, we are still enjoying sleeping outside away from the stench of the other men as well as all the snoring that goes on that would wake the dead. The tent ain't nothing fancy and I am guessing it is left over from the war but it meets our needs and we can pack it up in a hurry and stow it in the car if we need to.

Some of the men off my work crew stop by to share some food and gossip about the things that are going on around the shantytown and among the gangs. Ever so often we get a newspaper about the goings on back East but mostly it's the gossip that draws a lot of the fellas' here. We was still laughing about that scene Kiernan and his now wife put up a while back when she grabbed him by the ear and drug him off to see the traveling parson. It seems she is expecting again and as much as he complains, I think he likes being married to that big woman.

Hopping John came by the other day and cooked us up a mess of gumbo, yams and pone that when you looked at it, you would think one of the fellas' put him up to it as a joke on us. Granted, it ain't much to look at but it sure tasted good and we ate that with some buffalo steak that a hunter just killed that day. I felt like I was an Arabian prince after that meal, it was so good.

We got to talking, trying to figure out what we was going to do with ourselves. It was a Saturday and the workday was done but nobody wanted to go over to shantytown 'cause that is a quick way to lose all the money a body earned from the week before. The good young Catholic lads still in their teens who just arrived from back East especially didn't wish to go on account of the whores always recognize the newcomers and target them first. They frequently get rolled by those hard hearted women or their pimps.

"Tell us a story, lads," Quinn jokingly prodded the young boys.

"What kind of story?" one of them replied.

"Whatever you like," Quinn said with a grin on his face. "Tell these lads a story about Finn McCool or Cuchullain or the like."

"Who?" they said with a puzzled expression.

"Don't tell me you daft little eegits don't know who Finn McCool or Cuchullain are," blustered Quinn. "You have to be pulling me leg that you know so little of your heritage."

The blushed look that passed over their faces, their cowering attempt to hide their shame, confirmed what everyone already knew.

"Jesus, Joseph and Mary," Quinn disgustingly replied as he looked toward heaven, crossing himself. "Wha's to become of the Irish if the likes of these lads are to keep our heritage alive? You are a shame, the lot of you. Did you know how important the telling of a tale is for the Irish? Why, back in the days of the Romans, the Irish were sent there to listen in on the Senate and re-tell the debates for those doing the recording. And the Hibernians had to meet out in the fields in order for us to learn the stories of our Catholic faith 'cause we weren't allowed to write none of it down."

The boys shook there heads no as Quinn's indigination subsided.

"All right, sit down the lot of you whilst I tell the story of Cuchullain," Quinn said with a resigned sense of disgust.

Quinn is a gifted story teller and loves an audience when he goes on about the stories of the homeland. I suspect his indignation was more of an act to coerce an audience than real anger.

We all gathered round the fire while he told the story of the bravest Irish warrior that ever lived, a young lad by the name of Sétanta who wanted to join the order of the Red Knights.

One day a fellow named Culann, a smith, invites the King of Ulster to dinner and on the way the king sees Sétanta out playing hurling with the other lads. The king is so impressed with Sétanta, he invites him to the big feast as well. Sétanta says he will follow along as soon as he finishes the game. Forgetting all about it, the king travels on and Culann, sets out his fierce guard dog to keep an eye out for trouble. Along comes Sétanta later to the feast and that dog commences to try to rip him to bits. Even though he is a little guy, he fights and kills the ferocious dog.

Well, Culann is upset by the boy killing his dog but everyone knows he did it in self-defense. Being the honorable boy that he was, Sétanta promises Culann that he will raise him another dog but in the meantime, he will guard the smith's house hisself. This impresses the king even more and a druid comes along and renames the boy Cuchullain which means 'Culann's hound' in the Irish. Cuchullain goes on to fight all kinds of battles and wins them all.

Quinn kept on with the stories of Finn McCool, the little people and so forth and who should want to tell a story of the old country but Hopping John hisself.

"My people come from West Africa," he said "We got stories and tales just like you Irish folk do about brave warriors and men who know the spirits."

Nobody said a word to him but it was clear by the hushed response, all were waiting to hear a tale unlike that which we had heard before.

Hopping John kept going in a hushed voice that made you lean forward whilst he was doing the telling. He told us the story about why ants are able to carry so much weight around. This is a good story for a bunch of teamsters and track layers which maybe the reason he thought of it.

Anyway, Kweku Anansi and Kweku Tsin, father and son were farmers who were starving on account of there was no rain. Tsin was walking along one day, very sad that he didn't have any crops when he came along a dwarf sitting by the side of the road.

The dwarf asked him why he was so sad and he told him his crops were getting ruined. The dwarf told him to fetch two small sticks and tap him on his humped back. Sure enough, he did and the dwarf said a spell and it commenced to rain.

The father, Anansi wanted to know how Tsin did it and he told him all about the dwarf. Being a clever type, the father did the same thing walking around pretending to be sad. He came across the dwarf and he told him tap him on his hump with two small sticks and he would cast a spell and make it rain. Anansi thought if I hit this dwarf with some really big sticks, we are going to get a lot of rain. He got him some whoppers and started wailing on the back of that poor dwarf. Well, that dwarf died and the king of the country got real mad at Anansi. He said he was going to have to carry around that dwarf in a box on his head for the rest of his life.

Anansi before long got real tired of carrying around that dwarf 'cause he was getting very heavy after a while. As he was walking about, he asked the ant, who was an honest fellow if he would hold the box for him for a while. The ant suspected it was a trick but since he had a high sense of honor, said he would do it until he got back. Of course, Anasi never returned and that is why we see ants able to carry large bundles wherever they go.

"I guess we's the ants in that story," opined Hopping John to which the rest of the crew shook their heads in agreement.

Hopping John told a few more stories and the tales kept going back and forth all night long with between him and Quinn telling stories of the old country, heroes and villains, fairy tales and such. They both knew how to spin a story and we never did get tired of the way they went on about Africa and Ireland. I wished I could remember stories better or I would tell them myself. I had to write these down or else I would forget them or get one story mixed up with another.

JM

Sunday

Today is Sunday and I feel almost ashamed of myself for sleeping nearly 'til mid-morning. I guess I am so tired from all the work during the week and from all the story telling the last night, I didn't think nothing of it. It was Quinn's snoring that woke me up and he don't usually make a lot of noise but he must be awfully tired also 'cause he was sawing away at some logs loud enough to wake all those back in Omaha.

I got to thinking about Hopping John's stories last night and they ain't so different from the yarns we spin about the Irish or the fairy tales that started in this country either. There is a lot about Hopping John I admire, more so as I have gotten to know him that it surprises even me.

Back before the war of the rebellion, I didn't think a whole lot about the Negroes 'cause first we didn't see a whole lot of them in Philadelphia. We heard a lot about them from the street agitators, especially as the war got closer. Usually those folk went to the Protestant churches and would go on and on about how evil slavery was and how wrong it was to hold a man in bondage. A lot of these folk were English abolitionists who would blather on about how they ended slavery in the English Empire and how it should stop in this country.

I remember my Ma and my sister Mary and all the old folks I knew in our old neighborhood calling all these street agitators a bunch of hypocrites. They would talk up freeing the slaves in this country but not lift a finger to feed a starving Irishman back in the old country. They would say how great their mission from God was to lift up the Negro but it was these same people who pushed downed the Irishman, allowing no man of the Catholic faith to own property, vote or other things people in this country take for granted. Some of the protestant pastors in Philadelphia would even go so far as to call the Irish and our faith a plague upon the nation which ended causing some very hard feelings, even some fights in the streets.

I reckon I didn't care one way or another if all the darkeys had their freedom or not when the war started. I changed my mind when the 116th started making their way through the Southern states and I started to see things different. We didn't live all that good in South Philadelphia but no man should have to live like the Negroes did on some of those plantations. Some of them had their backs whipped so bad from all the beatings they took, it was one big mass of scars. Others had their children pulled away from them so they could be sold off to someone else. James, Mary and I leastwise got to be with our ma up to the day she died.

I am sometimes sad for the Negroes in the South and for the Indians in these parts. I didn't have nothing to do with their troubles but I understand why they might be so angry at the white man for telling him how they got to do things. We Irish are white and we still have people telling us what to do in our own country.

Hopping John changed all the ideas I had about Negroes that I had before the war. He is a smart man and one of the most upstanding people I ever knew. He can work all day harder than any two white men put together. He can fight any four men and whip them all at the same time yet every time I see him with my dog Colleen, he is gentle as he can be.

Many of the men around here don't see that in Hopping John, especially those who don't know him. All they see is a huge Negro with a holey grey hat. I wish they could see him on the inside though like I finally have. I am sure they would want him as someone to call their friend as I have.

JM

French Photographs

Today a fight nearly broke out in the dining hall which would have been quite a ruckus if it had got going full bore. When we go in to eat, we sit at these really long tables, one man next to another. This ain't no fancy affair by any means with so many men packed in there together and if one man takes a swing at another, he is likely to connect with someone else by accident, gettin' that fella involved.

Anyway, back to the story. Me and Quinn was standing in line to get our food and we noticed that one table was passing around some cards and I thought that was mighty strange for men to get all excited over some cards. There was even some whistling at some of the cards and I knew straight off these couldn't be no ordinary cards.

We sat down the next table over and I heard the boys talking, "I like that one," and "Ain't she a beauty," and "I would swim all the way to France for that girl."

"What's that you are looking at that has the lot of ya' stretching your necks out like a turtle on a hot rock?" asked Quinn.

"This photographer came through here the other day and sold us some pictures of French ladies he took when he was in Paris. These women pretty much show off all their worth," said one of the younger looking fellows.

"You don't say," says Quinn. At that, the younger of the crew flashed one of the photos Quinn's direction to show he was quite serious in his assertion.

"What would a little spud like yourself be doing with a woman like that?" asked Quinn with a wry smile. "Your mammy just barely let you wear trousers and you thinking yourself all grown up and ready to show this French woman how to make love. It is a big difference between kissing a sheep and kissing a woman, boy-oh."

Quinn's insult landed solid on the poor boy and his mates broke out in riotous laughter. The poor boy, maybe barely sixteen, turned red in the face as though he had been shamed by the bishop himself. His face downcast, one of the lads pulled the photo from his hand and said, "You'll not be needing that. There is a herd of sheep over in shantytown. Maybe we can get you a photo of that," to which the boy's mates laughed all the harder.

"Give that back!" the boy shouted at which the other lad held the photo high over his head. He kept crowding the other boy not thinking of what he was doing or who he was crowding. "Give that back!" he repeated.

The one kept backing up holding the photo high with the other kept advancing, trying to get the picture. Soon, the backing one tripped and fell over one of the long tables while the other lad trying to retrieve his photo landed square on top of him, collapsing the table and causing the food of all the men to cover them and the floor with portions of meat, beans, potatoes and spilled coffee.

The two lads had a look of horror on them as they glanced up at their very angry colleagues who were shaking bits of food, gravy and coffee off their clothes and out of their beards. One of the men at the table, John O'Brien, a solid stoic type, stood there silently staring at the two.

"That will be enough of that," John finally said between his teeth. He grabbed the young lad who was trying to retrieve his photo of the French woman by the ear and pulled him toward the door with the lad squirming behind. John held a firm grip on him as the walked steadily to the door, grabbed him by the scruff of the neck and kicked him in the arse, out the door and onto the ground.

The other knew his turn was coming had already made for the door hoping to escape having his ear nearly torn out of his head like his friend or getting a kick in the arse. He was not fast enough for O'Brien. You could hear the thud of O'Brien's boot on the lad's butt as he made his escape, but for naught. O'brien lifted him cleanly in the air and he landed a good eight feet away, face down in the dirt to the laughter of the men waiting in line to get their food.

Both of those boys didn't bother dusting themselves off or turn around to see if he was coming. They just lifted themselves off the ground and started running in different directions, hoping O'Brien wouldn't come after them.

As O'Brien turned to re-enter the dining hall, he was met with the claps and cheers of approval from his fellow workers. O'Brien doffed his hat with a smile and the line parted to allow him to return to the front to get another helping of food with extra portions this time around. A seat opened up for him at a nearby table with the men slapping him on the back and congratulating him on his handling of the matter.

I turned to see if the lad's mates were still at the table near us but they excused themselves and slipped out the door when nobody was paying attention. Quinn turns to me and says, "Now what do you think their hurry was? They left their food just where it was."

That Quinn has a wicked sense of humor but regardless, I enjoy it nonetheless.

JM

Photographers and Journalists

It seems we can't turn around these days without stepping over a newspaper reporter or photographer from back East who wants to get the story about what's going on out here building the railroad. They are always asking questions among the men about how much track we laid, are the Indians bothering us and when will it be done and on and on.

I don't mind so much but some of them can be downright intrusive. You might be working along holding something heavy and before you know it, they are right in your way when you need to lay a rail down or swing your hammer. One reporter asked to put down a rail with the crew and another swing the hammer just to see how much it weighs.

One came up to me and Quinn and was telling us that everybody back East is talking about nothing else but the western railroad. Mr. Greely's paper in New York always has some news about the railroad and the reporter from that paper brought out some extra copies to share with the workers which were greatly appreciated from the men who know how to read. After the work day, I read some of the stories going on back East and what they was saying about us in the *Herald*. The stories they were writing made the men real proud of themselves and they kept asking if there were any more stories about the railroad. I kept reading for them until my voice wore out and then someone else took over. By that time, I had done read all of the stories there was to tell from that paper about us.

Photographers are coming around too but they don't bother the men nearly so much. They usually stand off at a distance and take pictures of us while we are working but sometimes they have us hold still pretending to work so the picture don't get blurred while he has the lens cover off. One thing for sure, we ain't much to look at cause most the men haven't taken a bath or washed their clothes in quite some time. If we know a photographer is coming around, some of the fellas might shave and take the time to get gussied up. I wouldn't mind sitting for a portrait but I got no place to put it right now so it don't get tore up. Besides, it costs more money than I care to spend anyhow. With all the photographers walking around here, I am sure I got my picture taken by several of them by now.

Besides taking pictures of us, they like to take pictures of the land. This is probably a good thing because I don't expect people back East can really understand what the West looks like until they see it for themselves or see it in a picture. Even if you do see things in a picture, the scale and size don't really come through. When you see a picture of a buffalo, you don't really see how big they are but when you are right next to them, they make you feel downright small. One thing the photographers take a lot of pictures of that are smaller than it seems are the Indians. A lot of times they will put the Pawnee braves in some warrior costumes to scare the people back East but the truth is they are not a very big people. Folks when they first arrive and don't know them get scared real easy thinking they are ten feet tall because they think all Indians are the same but they ain't. The Pawnees have been helping us a lot fighting off the Sioux and Cheyenne 'cause they understand they way those other tribes think.

One good thing about all these reporters and photographers coming out here is they will put something down so everyone can see how this thing was done and put together. On the one hand we are rushing through trying to get this job done as quick as we can because there is so many people in this country who want to see the nation joined together by rail. On the other hand, we build a lot of bends and switchbacks in the line that are not necessary so those backing the railroad financially get more money per mile. It don't matter to me if we build it in circles as long as they pay me my wage but eventually we will have to meet them coming from California someplace.

Another thing about these reporters is they add more words to a sentence when you are talking with them than you can follow. It seems some of them like to hear the sound of their own voice and will rattle off a soliloquy from Shakespeare or such to impress the fellows. It don't impress nobody here because the men have grown accustomed to using few words when talking with one another and when you hear a man using so many words, you wonder if he is some fop or dandy. That is usually not the case but the men here get a strange look in their face when someone starts talking and carrying on so. I almost started laughing the other day when one started carrying on and had the airs of an English lord. One of the men threw a shovel full of dirt and hit him in the backside and pretended it was an accident and begged the man's pardon. That fellow walked away in a snit, swatting at his own backside and shaking his legs trying to get the dirt to fall out of his trousers. If those fellows ain't good for nothing else, they are at least good for a laugh when the lads want to play a practical joke on someone.

JM

We break our record

General Jack told me and some of the other foreman that he wanted to have a race today to see how much track the crews could lay in a day. It seems Mr. Crocker of the Central Pacific has been blustering about how much his Chinamen could do and Mr. Durant had is pride hurt, saying his Irishmen could lay more track and was prepared to prove it.

Now I don't mind a race and every good Irishman loves the competition but I don't want to see my men get hurt for no good reason, especially since I have a crew that works very well together. Still, when General Jack told me if we could lay more than four miles of track today, he would offer each man on our crew double, maybe triple wages and a pound of tobacco each. Well, there would be no way I could contain that information and my men would be sure to hear of it and be cursing me to the nether reaches if I didn't take him up on the offer.

"We'll get it done," says I to General Jack. "But I will be wanting to lay out the supplies, water, fishplates and such at key intervals along the grade so we don't have to send someone back to fetch them."

"Consider it done, McGlinchey," says General Jack.

I bid him good day and turned to walk away. Soon I found my men sipping on their morning coffee and told them about the wager, the work and the bonuses should we succeed. I threw out the challenge and asked them if they were up for it and they gave me a hearty chorus of agreement.

"Good," says I. "Then let's get started."

It was not quite sun-up yet but the activity in the camp was the same as it might be during mid-day with crews preparing for the daily work, teamsters harnessing their animals and loading the wagons with supplies. I told the men to gather their hammering mauls, tongs and whatever else they might need for the day.

The time we would work it was decided would be from sun up to sun down. The morning twilight was breaking over the horizon and soon the sun would creep up just beyond the last stretch of prairie. I told the foreman to give us the time when the sun came up and I would give the order for the men to start laying the track.

At 6: 04 a.m., the sun popped up over the horizon and I gave the order for the men to commence. The tenders rolled out the rails from the wagons at a near run, picking up each with their tongs and waddling out to the last rail that had been laid down like some geese holding a 600 pound piece of metal amongst them. The way they walk is how those fellows got the name gandy dancers cause they look like 'ganders doing a dance' and the name stuck. Anyway, the lead tender gave the word, "Drop" and the men placed the rail with near precision in the exact place it needed to be. The gauger would hold the measuring rod across the rails right quick to see if the distance was just right and it nearly always was 'cause the men could eyeball the distance by now to within an inch or two of where it needed to be. Soon as the men made the adjustment and the rail dropped into the right place, the spikers would come along and drive those iron nails into the timbers beneath with just three stroke of the maul. All the time that is going on, fellows that are nimble with their hands are putting the fish plates on that hold the two sections of track together, bolting and turning those nuts in place to make sure they are firmly tied together.

Lucky for us it was a cloudy day and we had a gentle breeze blowing throughout giving the men some relief. I don't think it would have mattered because the men's pride was involved in this and damn the sun and the flies and whatever else, we were going to get those four miles today if it killed us. The men worked steady, getting a rhythm together that was not hurried but there was no wasted motion either. No person was ever idle except when I put a man to substitute for another so he could get something to drink or a meal in him. We rotated men in and out of the crew for both the noon time meal and for supper.

About eleven in the morning, word got out that we were trying to make four miles and some of the reporters and photographers came by to get a look at us while were laying the track. I told them I don't mind them looking on but don't be getting in the way, don't be asking us to stand still whilst they take their photographs and don't talk to the men as they are working or one of them might get hurt 'cause they ain't paying attention. They came out to admire us and many nodded their approval at our efforts and thankfully, gave us enough room to do the work we needed to get done.

By three in the afternoon, I knew by the rail count we had laid over two miles of track but I didn't tell the men. I wanted them to continue on with the pace they had been keeping which was pretty steady throughout the day. One of the men who was acting as a substitute tender dropped the rail on his foot and might have broke it. The man who he was substituting for finished off his water and got right back into laying the track without missing a beat and we sent that fellow back up the track to the infirmary with one of the teamsters who was bringing us some supplies.

At six in the evening, the sun started casting long shadows on the prairie and I knew we would be close. The rail count had us over three miles and I urged the men to continue on because the sun would be down soon.

"Come on boys, tomorrow is Sunday and you will have all day to rest," I urged. "You going to let that blowhard Crocker speak that way against an Irishman."

A chorus of denials came my direction and the men forgot about their weariness, at least for the time being and started working just a bit faster, picking up the pace in a visibly measurable sense. I was glad they were willing to put out the extra effort and I hoped it would last until sundown which looked like it might come in another hour or so. The hammering of the mauls were like a steady 'clink, clink' clink' of a precise time piece.

Soon the sun started edging toward the horizon and the men on the crew started to make note of its position in the sky without missing a beat on the maul or the laying of a rail. They just glanced toward the horizon and kept steadily trudging forward as did I. A crowd of men from the crew came along with reporters and others who wanted to look on to see if the men would meet their goal. People started cheering them on from the side of the tracks which seemed to lift the spirits of the men, some worked even harder to increase the rate of track laid. "Come on boys, you can do it." "Four miles men, four miles." "To hell with Crocker, boys," all said over the continuous clinking of mauls pounding the spikes into the rails, clang of the fishplates slapped against the rails and huffs and rasping heaves of the tenders and they waddled their iron into place.

The men were dripping with sweat and to their credit, only took water when they couldn't hold out any more. The intensity only increased the closer the sun got to the horizon until finally, the foreman shouted out in a very loud voice, 'Time, gentlemen'.

The men dropped their mauls and wheezed to gather their breath. None sat but only looked to the foreman for the answer that everyone wanted to know, 'how much track got laid'.

The foreman who was joined by General Jack knew what the men wanted to know as did the rest of the crowd by the looks on their faces. It had to be good because General Jack was grinning ear to ear. The foreman looked into the crowd and said, "According to the number of rails laid today, this crew has broken its own record by laying four miles and two hundred yards of iron."

General Jack and the foreman were about to offer their congratulations but their words were cut short from the shouts of hurrahs going up into the air from the crowd and the men who had been laying the track throughout the day. To look at those fellas', you would think that they hadn't been doing a thing all day after the announcement. Several began dancing a jig with the crowd clapping their hands in time. Those men began to dance around the side of the track grinning broad smiles and to the laughter at all who watched their show.

One well wisher off to the side threw out a bottle of whiskey which was deftly caught in the air by one of the crew. He took a swig and passed it on to the fellow standing next to him. I was hungry and tired and just wanted to wash up and go to sleep. "Four miles," I thought to myself. I jumped on back of a teamster's wagon that was heading back to camp followed by Hopping John and Quinn. We didn't say nothing and didn't need to say anything. Once back in camp, I fell on my cot and didn't wake until late morning the following day.

JM

1868 - News from the Catholic Herald

A couple of newspapers from back East came in today that the lads and I found very interesting, especially the Catholics among us. The *Catholic Herald*, a newspaper put out by the Church, and another one that appeals to the Irish, the *Irish American*, came in neatly tied bundles for us to read and pass among the men. Granted, the news is very old, some issues several weeks at the earliest and several months, the oldest, but it is still fine to be hearing stories about our people back east and in the old country.

There was an editorial in the *Herald* written by a bishop about the necessity of temperance among the Irish that was read aloud to the laughter of most of the men. Some of the more devout fellows gave a scolding for the blasphemy of those who ridicule the church and the good priests who look over us.

Hoppin' John whispered to me, "Why does the white man carry on so with the liquor?"

"I honestly don't know," I replied. And I don't. It seems the drink is the curse of the Irishman but the way they think about it, almost as necessary as water.

Even my dog Colleen has more sense that a lot of my countrymen. One fellow threw up from a night of drinking and she went over to get a smell because it was bothering her so. She yelped and curled her tail between her legs and came trotting over to me and moved between my legs, it repulsed her so.

Men don't have a lot to do out here once the work is done and that leads to all kinds of mischief, especially when every corner you turn away from the camp is offering you a drink and a woman for a day's wage. Once the man begins to drink, it takes no time at all for all his money to leave him and he starts over the next day, swinging his hammer or shoveling dirt in the hole and with him owing $5 for his room and board.

My brother wrote me that back in Philadelphia, the temperance unions are growing all the more popular among our people which is hard for me to imagine. I remember when I was a little lad walking down Spofford street in Moyamensing near the banks of the river, you would often have to step over the men who had too much of the drink the day before. Yet, according to my brother, all kinds of social events are sponsored by the temperance agitators. Parishes are setting up social events like dancing and picnics that allow no alcohol to be served at all. These temperance workers are helping our people with problems beside the drink as well including setting up committees to help with immigration, libraries and reading rooms at the parish. A reading room out here sounds a bit queer to the ears but would be welcome since anything to read is gobbled up like a piece of meat set before a hungry dog.

Philadelphia seems like such a distant place now. Now that I have been traveling about the country, I don't think I can stop. Going throughout the South when I was droving cattle for the quartermasters allowed me to see a lot of areas of the country that I never thought I would see when I was a young lad.

I never had a thought in my head about doing that until my sister died when I was fifteen and had no one to look after me. I was old enough to work but too young to fight and the war was on so off I went riding drag and pushing herds of cows wherever there was fighting and feeding men to be done.

It's too bad my mother and sister died at such an early age but it is the Lord's will I reckon. I would like to have shown them this country and I am sure they would have loved it in spite of the risk from the Indians. My brother tells me he is considering riding the train to California and settling there once we have this railroad built. He is tired of his job, of paying his landlord for the rent of his room and how crowded Philadelphia is becoming. He is thinking of moving near Los Angeles and buying a small bit of land to call his own. Says he wants to pick and eat oranges off his own tree. I told him he should even though we haven't made it to California yet and I don't know nothing about it except what I heard. If it is half as good as the rumors you hear, then it should be a fine place indeed.

The truth is I don't know where I belong anymore. I traveled all over the South during the war but I still have an urge to keep moving. Pa died back in the old country and as long as the English own our lands, we have no part in our own country. Ma and Sister Mary are both gone now, died of the cholera, having been buried at St. Joseph's parish. My brother is telling me he wants to move to California. I suppose there is more traveling to be done, money to earn and maybe some day finding a wife to settle down with. Then

I can think of things like that but for now, my place is here out on the prairie with the men on my crew.

JM

Cheyenne, Wyoming – Teaching Hoppin' John

We have been having a devil of a time trying to get back to work with the late winter and early spring rains tearing up everything we have built. Just as soon as we think that we are going to get a break, the rains come roaring in and start all over. Many of the grades that were set up have pretty much washed away.

Worse yet, the swollen rivers have tore up a good part of the bridges the engineers built back east and now they have to be done completely over. Ferrying supplies across the river has become a risky venture as well since we lost a gang of men and a team of mules trying to make it across. Sadly these men drowned and when the men got word of it, the whole camp mourned terribly. I expect I would hate to be drowned and word is when these men realized they couldn't fight against the river, the expression on their faces was one of panic and terror. They knew they were going to die and there was nothing anyone could do for them except watch them be swept away. Men called out to them to hang on but it was no use. They were found later washed up on the bank. General Jack and Mr. Dan had a burial service for the men which most of us attended.

Since things have been so slow, I have been teaching Hoppin' John a little bit more about reading and ciphering. He catches on real quick and he knows all his letters by sight now and can even write his own name. I showed him how to add and subtract so he don't get cheated when he goes to the shantytowns to buy something or he knows how much money he has coming to him when the paymaster's car comes to give us our wages. He has been holding pretty much all of his on account but sooner or later he is going to want his money, for what he hasn't said yet but I expect he will want a place of his own as well to settle down. One place he told me he ain't going is back down South cause some of the old Confederates have been pretty hard on the former slaves, especially on those who they think are getting uppity.

Hoppin' John mentioned that General Sherman has been sending out handbills and recruiters trying to get Negroes to fight the Indians. He said he is giving it some thought 'cause he always has admired the soldiers from the first time he saw them coming through Georgia during the war. The Indians got a special name for them and call them Buffalo Soldiers since their head is so wooly like that of a buffalo and because they can be pretty fierce in a fight as well.

I expect Hoppin' John would make a pretty good soldier 'cause he is a pretty tough man, adaptable and fearless. I am pretty sure the Indians who tangled with him would get more than they bargained for. Some of the smarter Negroes become sergeants and such I think if he keeps up learning the way he does, he will be able to read on his own account before it's all over with.

It's funny how Hoppin' John is with learning. He said it was against the law for a slave to learn reading and writing when he was a boy. Some of the men when they see me teaching him how to read ask Hoppin' John, "What use does a darky have for reading and writing anyhow?" I tell them, "less flies will go into your mouth ifin you keep it shut" or "mind you own business and keep moving." Hoppin' John don't say nothing and just keeps sounding out the words ever so slowly. He gets a big smile on his face when he gets it right and always seems ready to try again. "One day I am going to read the Bible," says he, "cover to cover. First I got to get me some money to buy me one first." I hope he does.

I remember when Father Costigan was teaching James and me to read back at St. Joseph's in Philadelphia. Mary our sister was off working and she wanted to be sure we stayed out of mischief. She took us by the hand down to the parish to meet Father Costigan and he was a giant of a man. All the boys in the class were quiet for fear of the Father turning around and giving them the look that I would later learn put the fear of eternal damnation in you.

I remember him saying over and over, "Just because you are poor is no reason to be ignorant, boy-oh. Now recite me those verses in Latin again." The Lord help you if you came to school unprepared. He would not stand for such nonsense. Still, the Father had a gentle side to him as well. When Mary died, he brought

James and me the news that the last rites were given before she passed. He knew we were still boys who needed looking after and found James a job working for the rail yard and I went to work droving cattle on my own accord.

I wonder how he is doing. I think I will write him a letter and give him some of the news that is going on out west. Maybe he has some to share from the old neighborhood.

JM

March 1868 – President Johnson's impeachment trial begins

We got word today that the Senate has put President Johnson on trial for 'high crimes' against the country. I don't reckon he done anything that bad as the charge implies except stand up to those idiots in the Senate and tell them all he ain't kowtowin' to none of them.

Ever since Mr. Lincoln got shot, those Senators have been out to get Mr. Johnson one way or another. That ain't the worst of it because they still want to give the South a beatin' even though the war is over and they are making life so miserable for those folks. General Sherman and his kind burned down or took everything of value when they went through and now those politicians want to make sure that the South won't be able to support itself by taxing their property during the war years and then taking away their property when they can't pay. On top of that, any man who fought for the South ain't allowed to vote so they can't make their voice heard in their own governments.

Even though most of the Irish fought for the North during the rebellion, we can sympathize with those people in the South. We are a dispossessed people as well with foreigners living on our lands in the old country. Some of those Southern folk are still making trouble for the occupying troops but who wouldn't want foreigners out of their country?

I am hoping Mr. Johnson gets through this mess all right. If he doesn't, those Radicals will run roughshod over anybody that gets in their way.

JM

April 1868- Cheyenne

The winter in Wyoming seems about over as the snow shows signs of melting almost everywhere. It rains from time to time with a little freezing on the ground but nothing that lasts very long. I saw some buds on a tree today which is an encouraging sign that spring is just around the corner.

That is all right with me because I am going stir crazy. It seems every two bit gambler, pimp, hustler and no account of low moral character has descended on this place looking to make a dollar with the least amount of effort possible. Stealing, cheating and even murdering to earn their living is as normal as breathing for some of these people and the sooner me and my crew starts building tracks that lead away from here, the better.

I talked with General Jack the other day and he thinks we should be on the move any day now. We have got a long way to go to the Pacific and he has in mind for us to cross the deserts of Utah by the end of the year. It seems the Central Pacific is still stuck in the mountains of the Sierra Nevada which is all right by General Jack by the look on his face when he told me.

Hoppin' John told me he doesn't think he is going to go any further than Cheyenne because he has made up his mind to enlist in the Army so that he can join up with the other Buffalo Soldiers. Says he likes the idea of a riding with other Negro soldiers and he hopes he might get the chance to be a sergeant. I think that he just might, considering how smart he is. Hoppin' John and I spent a lot of time practicing reading this last winter and he is doing real well. He can write his name and he read me some stories from the Chicago paper. Granted, he reads slower than molasses in January but still he is getting better every day. I will sit down next to him sometimes and bring him some old newspaper and point to this story or that and ask him to read it aloud to me and my dog Colleen. He don't hesitate one bit and picks up the paper and away he goes, telling me about what woman is engaged to what man, what the politicians are doing in Springfield and so forth. Colleen sure likes Hoppin' John cause he always has an ear scratch for her and sometimes he will dig out a piece of jerky for her and throw it in the air for her to catch.

Before he goes soldiering against the Indians, he asked me to come down with him when he swears in and I said I would. I want to see him off and I think Quinn wants to come along as well. There is still a lot to do here on the prairie as far as getting the red man on the reservation.

Most of the Indians don't cotton to the idea of leaving the life they know to go live on a worthless piece of land that the white man sets aside for him. Indian agents are all the time stealing their provisions. Learning farming, blacksmithing or some other trade is a foreign idea for these fellows who have always been hunters and warriors. Still, as sad as the situation is for them, they have got to get on those reservations or they will all get killed by the soldiers or starve because the railroad is hiring men all the time to go out and kill as many buffalo as they can.

I did pretty good this winter holding on to my wages and didn't spend hardly any money at all beyond the room and board. There were all kinds of temptations around here as I said but after a while, they all seem the same. It seems like the same people are always trying to get you that first drink for free to get you mixed up with them but as long as you don't take that first step in, you will be fine.

I can't say that is the case with most of the fellows around here as they have got themselves all balled up with some bad people. Many a bunk in my place has been cleared out by the foreman 'cause they got themselves stabbed, shot or beat up so bad, they had to be moved to the infirmary while they healed up.

Luckily most of my crew are wise to that nonsense which is why I brought them in the first place. They don't take to the drink like so many of the lads from the old country.

If there was ever a curse placed on our people, it is this; the weakness for the drink. So many a good man has been ruined by the taking of spirits. It seems Satan knew the Irish would take over the world so he put a bottle of whisky in front of them telling them, "the first drink is on me," knowing that an Irishman would not be able to stop until the bottle was empty. Well, Lord thank you for giving me the sense to see through that lie by knowing my own Dad drink himself to death. He was a strong man except in that sense and sadly was frozen to death, found lying in a country lane with an empty bottle in his hand.

Not that I ever knew my Pa 'cause we left the old country when I was three but Mary my sister always said I am the spitting image of him. I remember Ma telling me that too but I don't remember Ma as much on account of she dying when I was barely nine years old and she always off working whilst my sister Mary took care of James and I.

One of the lads who works on another crew came to Quinn and told him that somebody around town was asking about him and me and where we could be found. Nobody in the saloon knew who we were so the fellas they asked said they didn't know the name and off the man went. Quinn's friend didn't let on because anybody who knew us also knew where to find us. That is mighty odd but I can't imagine what they would want 'cause I don't know anyone outside the works crews that would know the both of us. The only people I can think of who might know me is someone from the Pennsylvania 116th Regiment I rode with during the war and is trying to look me up. Still, until I get a better idea who it might be, I keep an eye peeled and keep Colleen nearby just in case. JM

Mid April 1868 – Near Dale Creek, Wyoming Territory

This morning when I was standing in line to get some food to eat I heard some men talking in front of me about a Negro man who got killed last night in shantytown along with his dog. I didn't think nothing of it at first because I don't know any darkies around here outside of Hoppin' John and I for sure didn't know any that had a dog.

"So what if a Negro man got killed last night," I was thinking to myself. People getting killed around here happens all the time, especially people that wander over to shantytown when they shouldn't.

Still, the thought wouldn't go away from me and I was bothered with it until about mid morning. I hadn't seen Colleen this morning and I figured she was off chasing rabbits or something that dogs like to do when there is good hunting. She sometimes did that but she always returned sometime during the day either at the work site or would be waiting for me when work was over underneath the railroad car out of the heat. Hoppin' John on

119

occasion didn't show for work but that was only when he wasn't feeling well and he told me he wasn't up to snuff lately. I asked Quinn about it and he said Hoppin' John told him he was going over there to get some elixir to pep him up a bit.

When he told me that I stood bolt upright. A cold sweat came over me and I dropped my tongs to the ground. I felt like I got been punched in the stomach, all the wind leaving my body and was unable to move. I got my wits about me and told the men to keep working and to find another fellow to fill in for me while I went to talk to General Jack.

I found General Jack straight away and asked his permission to go searching for my man. "He's not a drinker," says I "and I am a feared that something dreadful has happened to him."

General Jack gave his permission without reservation and I found me a horse and headed back up the line to the shanty town. I rode down a row of tents and came across one of the whisky peddlers that was milling about taking care of his business.

"Excuse me," says I. "One of my men has gone missing, a big darkey that stands well over six feet tall and has a barrel of a chest. You wouldn't miss him on account of his size and his holey gray hat that he never takes off. Have you seen him?"

"Yeah, I saw him. Got into a hell of a fight last night with some fellows I ain't never seen around these parts. I don't know the whole story but I saw the fight sure enough and he gave a good account of himself. They jumped him from behind and had his arms pinned behind his back. One of those fellows was closing in on him to cut him up with a knife. His dog got mixed up in it as well a snarling and a barking at those fellows who attacked him. That dog would have ripped a couple of those fellows arms clean off their bodies if one of 'em hadn't shot that cur. That darkey got mad then and threw those fellows like they was rag dolls. Just when I thought the darkey might beat the four of 'em, the one holding the knife ended pulling a gun and shot him dead as well."

"You know where I can find 'em?" I asked.

"Yeah, someone lassoed them and drug them to the edge of the camp. It's just over thataway," he gestured.

I didn't bother to thank the man because I wanted to see with my own eyes what I was starting to dread. I galloped over the couple of hundred yards following the drag marks to the edge of the camp. There in a heap face down was the body of a darkey and a dog, covered in dust. I pulled back hard on the reins and leapt from my horse. I ran over to the body and turned it upright. It was Hoppin' John. Next to him, covered in matted blood and dust was Colleen, both of them shot dead.

JM

June, 1868 - Laramie, Wyoming

This is the first time I have written in this journal in a while since Hoppin' John and Colleen got murdered over in the shantytown back up the track a couple of months ago. I been doing my work like always but I haven't felt much like talking with others 'cause I have been feeling so low. I haven't been staying in the sleeping car with the crew 'cause the weather has turned again and me and Quinn set up the tent for sleeping outdoors. Quinn and General Jack will often times give me a long look and ask me if everything is all right with myself and I always tell them I am fine. Quinn has been trying to get me to go out for ride on Sundays or play a game of cards with some of the lads off our crew but I ain't in the mood for nothing but sleeping. Most of Sunday is spent laying in my cot catching up on my sleep but Quinn nags me like Mary used to about it ain't natural for a person to sleep that much.

Anyway, the pace of our work has been picking up and we may have to work on Sundays as well. This shows me how determined General Jack is to make up for the slow pace we are going at now. I found a replacement for Hopping John but of course he can't do nearly the same amount of work he could. I reckon nobody on this crew could but that's another story. Everyday, I still expect Colleen to come out from under the sleeping car when I return home from work but she never does.

Me and our work crew held a little service for Hopping John back up the line and buried him alongside the track 'cause I don't think he would want to be buried in that trashy little shantytown. General Jack came by to show his respects and I appreciate him doing that and I think the other men on our crew did as well.

Our work has to go on and I guess it is time for me to stop moping around being sorry for myself.

We got some big problems on the work site a while back that got many a man scared, including me. General Jack has found himself in a tight spot with the construction of the rail on account of the terrain we have to go over. We were near a spot called Dale Creek which don't imply nothing of what it means. There is a huge gap of a canyon we have to get across and the engineers had been trying to come up with ideas about how it can be done.

One of them came up with the idea of building wooden trestles across the gap, built one on top of the other kind of like the Romans did with the aqueducts back in the ancient times. I ain't never seen an aqueduct but what I saw, it didn't appear steady enough for a man to walk across, much less a train. These fellas' were awfully clever however 'cause they built a bunch of reinforced wooden triangle looking things back up the line in Chicago, shipped out to here and set them in place almost perfectly fit.

Ain't nobody had confidence in that bridge 'cause it would sway in a strong wind and some of the men refused to go up there to lay track. One of the foremen went up there and called down to his crew that it was fine and there was nothing to worry about although I think he was trying to convince himself the whole time what he was saying was true. They got the bridge up and it measure over 120 feet high and was near 700 feet long. Of course they reinforced it with some steel cables tied to the bedrock below which helped out a lot but the trains still don't dare cross it when the wind is whipping up. The fastest they can go across now is just a snail's pace with a sign that tells the engineer not to go over four miles an hour.

Now we are at the town of Laramie. This place was laid out by the railroad and like a lot of the towns along the way has attracted every type of low life. There are some folks who seem to be getting mighty tired of that element and have formed a committee to clean out the undesirables. I don't know if it's a lot of talk but the town folk seem more committed to keeping this place free from whiskey peddlers, gamblers and pimps. I guess time will tell but by that time, we will hopefully be over the divide on our way to California.

JM

July 4, 1868

Today is Independence Day from the English, something that all Irishmen appreciate in our adopted homeland of America. We got the day off today to celebrate and most did so with an exuberance that can only match that seen in the St. Patrick's Day parades in South Philadelphia. General Jack came around and congratulated the men on a job well done since we have been laying track at more than a mile a day. True to his word, he gave out the tobacco he promised as a bonus.

The Army was showing off like only the Army can do when there is a patriotic celebration to present. A horse race among the soldiers was cause for every man on the crew to pick their favorite animal and rider and make their bets. Sgt. O'Halloran officiated the event with the officers, young and old looking on and sizing up the riders. O'Halloran held his pistol high above his head and after a nod from Major Stevens fired into the air. Horses snorted in a breath of air, the sound of ripping turf and galloping of hoofs over the prairie soon followed. Rebel yells and cheers from among the men urging their favorite rider on followed with hands cupped to their mouth, "Come on Denton, don't let me down," or "Run Buttercup, run, RUN..." Even the Indians in the camp seemed to be enjoying the race and you rarely see one of them smile but I could swear that I saw some of the braves downright enjoying the run. Private Simmons who rode Buttercup, a three year old gelding won the race. He is a fine horseman who before he joined the army had never been on a horse. Some were just born to do things and he and Buttercup made a fine pair.

After the race, the army fired some of the cannon in a 21 gun salute to the Union. This scared the Pawnees something terrible as old men and women went diving for cover underneath the wagons to the laughter of onlookers. They soon re-emerged with no change of expression after they saw that it safe to stick their heads out. Even the Southerners admired the cannon fire and fireworks but were pretty restrained otherwise. Union Soldiers who fought in the Vicksburg campaign lifted their glasses and remembered the day the city fell but to their credit, did not make a big to do of it in deference to the Southern soldiers who fought there as well.

Glasses were raised among the men as they milled about, praising the glories of the Union, Daniel O'Connell, the North, the South, girlfriends and wives back home, countries left behind and new territory to conquer, to the damnation of the savage who killed our men, the ruination of the English Empire, higher wages, shorter hours and blessings upon of General Lee. Before long, men were singing choruses of songs that were well known including the one that seemed to be a favorite of the men. It is called Poor Paddy on the Railway and it is about the Irish working man and his time spent laboring for the rails. Men sang this song over and over, the words becoming more slurred as the day wore on. I don't particularly like the tune but after hearing if for the better part of the day, I thought I might get it out of my head if I write it down.

Irish Gandy Dancer

Poor Paddy on The Railway

In eighteen hundred and forty one
Me corduroy breeches I put on
Me corduroy breeches I put on
To work upon the railway, the railway
I'm weary of the railway
Poor Paddy works on the railway
In eighteen hundred and forty two
From Bartley Pool I moved to Crewe
And I found meself a job to do
Workin' on the railway

I was wearing corduroy britches
Digging ditches, pulling switches, dodging hitches
I was workin' on the railway

In eighteen hundred and forty three
I broke me shovel across me knee
And went to work with the company
In the Leeds and Selby Railway

I was wearing corduroy britches
Digging ditches, pulling switches, dodging hitches
I was workin' on the railway

Irish Gandy Dancer

In eighteen hundred and forty four

I landed on the Liverpool shore

Me belly was empty, me hands were sore

With workin' on the railway, the railway

I'm weary of the railway

Poor Paddy works on the railway

In eighteen hundred and forty five

When Daniel O'Connell he was alive

Daniel O'Connell he was alive

And workin' on the railway

I was wearing corduroy britches

Digging ditches, pulling switches, dodging hitches

I was workin' on the railway

In eighteen hundred and forty six

I changed me trade from carryin' bricks

Changed me trade from carryin' bricks

To work upon the railway

The day was concluded with hilarity that only an Irishman with too much nerve can bring to a party coupled with one whisky too many. Maybe two or three too many. It seems that a fellow was bragging on his friend who would ride a cow down the middle of shantytown. Two Irish boys had just arrived from the East Coast never heard of such nonsense and decided they would each wager five dollars that no man could do such a thing. Shaking his friend awake, the four walked over to the cow pens and began looking for a suitable cow to do the job.

Unbeknownst to the Irish boys, this was all a con. The men had a cow already picked out that was quite tame and would readily accept a rider the size of this rather small man. The man straddled his cow who continued chewing it's cud without the least bit of bother. Spurring Old Bossy on, the cow walked through the gate and leisurely down the street with the Irish boys looking on with their jaws hanging loose. Men were cheering on the rider, some laughing, others pointing but for the most part, not getting a lot of attention because shantytown produces many sights that are hard for the eyes to accept and this was a minor one by comparison.

Realizing they were about to be separated from their hard earned wages, one of the Irish lads found a large splinter of wood from a stake and came up behind the cow, gave her a swift poke in the shank to which she reacted with the most violent manner, kicking up her heels and spinning around. The smaller con man did his best to hold on to old Bossy but it was no use. He went flying high and far and landed square into a pile of horse dung and muddy wash. The Irish boys disappeared into the night between the tents and a gathering laughing crowd. The con men were left trying to get control of a bucking, angry Bossy, tend their bruises and restore their wounded pride.

JM

Fort Sanders, Wyoming - General Grant comes for a visit

There was a lot of excitement in the camps when we were told that General Grant would be coming to pay a call on the workers here on the frontier. Men who fought for the Union couldn't wait to see the man in person who took the sword from General Lee. I never got to see the general myself when I was droving cattle for the Union but one of the men on my gang saw him on horseback when he was directing the battle of Richmond.

Some of the men who fought for the South wanted nothing to do with him, especially those who had lost family members during some of the sieges the General directed. Still, others seem resigned to let the war be in the past and something that can't be changed. You can see it by their willingness to joke with former Union soldiers about some of the things that occurred on the battlefield. This used to be a topic that men on the gangs didn't talk about for fear of starting an argument which in turn would lead to knives being drawn and one or both of the men getting stuck in the belly.

The day finally arrived and the train came in with bunting and flags draped all over the side of the cars and engines. General Grant walked out from the car to the platform to the shouts of 'Huzzah, huzzah, huzzah' from the former Union soldiers. The General was guarded by a detachment of cavalry and was surrounded by other important people that accompanied him on his campaign trip. One of the party I did recognize at once was

General Sherman, the man who made the march through Georgia, now running the Army west of the Mississippi and in charge of fighting the Indians on the frontier.

General Grant spoke to the very attentive crowd, telling us how proud he was of the work we were doing and how much this means to the future of the country. To continue with this important work, it was critical to elect him as the next President of these United States. He would see the frontier was made safe for future generations of Americans and to expand the railroad throughout other parts of the country.

Most of the men cheered at this while some of the Southerners passively listened to his speech. Some Southerners ain't allowed to vote anyway because they hadn't taken the loyalty oath and because their families back home would disown them if they did. Re-constructionists are pretty harsh in some areas of the South and I don't reckon I blame them about how they feel if half the stories they tell are true.

After his speech, General Grant came off the platform and began walking through the crowd, shaking hands and patting men on the back. Some of the men did the same, patting the General on the back in return and telling how grateful they were to him for this or that, telling short tales of their battles together and the General laughing or showing a somber face as the occasion called for. I held out my hand and the General took it and he quickly passed on to another man who was crowding in for the chance to see the famous man.

General Grant ain't too awfully tall, about 4 inches shorter than me; a stout man whose clothes seemed to hang very loosely about him. He smelled just a bit of whisky and cigars and seemed most sincerely amiable. Following behind him was General Sherman who also stirred up some excitement with his walk through the crowd. Some of the men shouted to him, "Good to see ya' again Uncle Billy," and "Did you come out here to give the Indians a whupping, Uncle Billy?" and so on. He smiled to the men but his job here was to build up his old friend General Grant so he played down the attention he got from his former comrades. General Sherman unlike General Grant had eyes that could turn a man to stone, so intense was his gaze. You could see straight away where the intensity he brought to the battlefield came from because it shown in his eyes unlike any man I had ever seen. If any Southerner had cause to bear a grievance against a Northern general, this is the one. I would not want to be an Indian off the reservation with General Sherman leading the fight.

Soon, General Grant bid farewell to all the men assembled, reminding us to vote Republican in the upcoming elections. "It is our duty to vote for progress," he reminded us. Soon, he disappeared into the crowd of people that moved as a bloc toward the waiting train. With one final wave and shouts of "Huzzah" in his ears, he turned his back on the crowd and the engine let off a shrill whistle and slowly the train moved off toward the next station back up the line.

JM

Green River, Wyoming – September, 1868

We have made it across the Wyoming territory and the work is getting harder all the time. Flat top mesas rise up out of the desert in vertical columns with practically no vegetation around us. Rock, rock and nothing but more rock is to be seen. Still, in its own way the landscape has an appeal to it and there is certainly nothing like it back East.

More and more visitors are coming out to have a look at the progress we are making toward joining the rail lines. General Jack for sure is getting tired of always having to show yet another group of dignitaries from back East around, ranging from Washington politicians to Yale professors gawking at a bunch of young men sling dirt in the middle of the desert. They make their judgments and pronouncements about the importance of this work, marvel at the landscape and the importance to the nation about building this great public work. When they talk with us we have a ready response for them that seems to make General Jack happy even though we know it tries his patience to have to entertain them when there is so much work to be done. Still, General Jack is a good host and to his credit never says a cross word to them even though I suspect he would if he were not a bit of a politician himself.

We are running out of wood to make cross ties for the rails and Mr. Dan seems concerned. We have to send back East for pretty near everything including water because there for sure ain't none to be had here. The graders continue to work the best they can in this heat but it is pretty hard even when everything is going right much less working in this furnace. We have to ration the water and men have been passing out from the heat, just dropping to the ground like limp rag dolls. Heck, even the mules can't take it sometimes and just the other day several died from the heat. This made Mr. Dan awful mad 'cause the drivers did not water them properly and replacing good mules costs a lot of money.

One feller who got too much of the heat keeled right over onto a big rock and did he ever have a knot on the side of his head when he woke up. Said he felt like a mule kicked him when he finally woke up and he laid under the wagon for a spell but General Jack told him to take it easy for a couple of days until he was back to his old self.

General Jack has been trying to get more workers out here because the work is getting so hard. He is rotating us in shifts working in the sun for a couple of hours at a time and then another group takes over while we rest and then the first group goes back to digging and so forth. Even with that we are exhausted at the end of the day because we can't get any rest at night either with the heat and flies never allowing us a minute's peace.

The dirt in this part of Wyoming is really fine and gritty and it leaves a white film over your whole body at the end of the day. Just walking over it kicks up a cloud that settles over everything, including the food and it seems we are always spitting dirt out to no avail. It would be fine to wash it off but there is no extra water to spare. Pretty near all of us use a cloth to cover our nose and mouth during the work day because that dirt gets in your nose and leaves large clumps of snot, making it hard to breathe. Several times a day, we have to take off our boots and turn them upside down to get rid of the gritty sand that finds its way in there despite our best to keep it out.

The iron is another problem we have to watch out for as well. Those rails heat up pretty quick during the day, especially when they are exposed to the sun for any length of time. I have been lucky and kept my wits about me before I get near one however a greenhorn that just arrived out here was not so lucky, grabbing the rail to show off and it burned him just the same as if it were a branding iron. He let out a yelp and started slinging his hand every which direction in order to cool it off but it was too late and the damage was done. He couldn't work with that hand any longer and it would be at least a week before he was able to return to work.

The miserable conditions here are causing tempers to be short especially among the new fellows just arriving from back East. I have been lucky enough to avoid getting in useless arguments with other men because I have developed a sense about who is on edge and who still has some rope to let out before the fists start flying. Most of the men I deal with are the same old group that I have been with since Nebraska and we have developed a good sense about the well being of each other without having to say it out loud.

I have to get some sleep but I am afraid it will be an exercise in futility. Already the heat shows no sign of letting up and the flies are making their rounds lighting on the men. I shall attempt to sleep nonetheless because a tired man is more likely to make a mistake, a mistake that in these parts may cost him his life if not careful.

JM

Utah – January, 1869

General Jack told me today we entered Utah today and it seems likely we will meet up with the California work gangs before long. We have been breaking our record it seems every other day with the amount of track we been laying because the terrain is so good and flat but now he seems particularly anxious to get even more done. Seems there is a bet between one of their big men and one of ours who can lay the most track before we meet up and our man ain't too anxious to lose or get his pride hurt. It don't matter to me none which of these millionaires lose their bet but I know the men on our gangs got a lot of pride in what they do and they want to keep beating their own record.

Hang the lot of those New York dandies for all I care but I ain't going to do nothing to see any of my men hurt toward the end of this thing. Of course I didn't tell Mr. Casement that but I assured him we would do the best we could and he of course promised bonuses for our men for each extra length of track that go laid over and above our quota. That for sure in itself will motivate our men to work extra hard cause soon this thing is gonna be over and we will have to take our wages and move on to the next bit of work, whatever that may be.

Speaking of that, Mr. Dan also told me that General Jack went to talk with Brigham Young, leader of the Mormons about hiring their men to do some grading work so that our side of the line will have more miles added on. That is both good news and bad news I guess. I know that will mean less work for us but the land our here is a might harsh. Dry, dusty and arid with a lot of cuts to be made.

I can say one thing for sure, this part of Wyoming and Utah is not where I will be staying for the rest of my days. The Mormons are more than welcome to this desolate place and if it gives them pleasure to worship out here among the snakes and scorpions, have it at I say. Some cattle drovers who came up not so long ago to bring our work crews some livestock have been talking a lot about Texas and Montana and how a man with a little money and lot of gumption could make a go of it. There is so much land they say that a man would have to ride a day or two to get to the nearest town if he had a mind to. Well, I don't need that much land but it sounds pretty good. I told one of them I used to drove cattle during the war and he assured me that I could hire on to an outfit no problem after I was done here. There are plenty of men who are putting together drives and a good man is always welcome if he is willing to pull his weight.

Wherever I go, I am going to need some new clothes pretty soon. These I got on me are wearing out and I am getting might tired of sewing on patches to hold them together. Maybe some new boots and a broad brimmed hat as well.

I checked my accounts here a while back and I got $474. 29 owed to me for my wages. I also have about eighty dollars in gold pieces on me but that's just in case I need to buy something right away. That is plenty to get you murdered over in the shantytowns if someone was to know you had that on you but I keep it hidden away, sewn inside my trousers. Dennis said he would pay me the $75 dollars I lent him for passage to get his family members here from Liverpool. I know he has that much on the accounts so when the paymaster's car comes he can pay me if I need the money he owes me.

I am off to a good start but after you figure in buying a good horse, saddle and sidearm and some new clothes, there ain't a whole lot of money left over to buy any land with, much less buy some lumber to build a house. I seen some of those soddies that those folks back in Nebraska were living out of and I don't want no part of that. I reckon I will have to save up a considerable amount more before I can get that place in Montana, Texas or even Timbuktu.

Quinn is talking about going to Nevada but he has in mind to do some mining. Like most Irish, he thinks that his fortune is one swing of a pick away from finding a silver vein that will keep him sipping French champagne and having a house like an English lord, full of servants to attend his every whim. I just listen to him blather on when he talks that way and I don't know if he believes himself or not. Maybe it's just a way to pass the day but the territory is full of Irish searching for their fortune and I expect if he follows after them, he will be just another digger in the mountains. He's got no ambitions that I know of except to get his family over from the old country and out west.

James ain't written in a while and I am hoping he is getting ready to move out to California when this railroad is complete. It shouldn't be long now and I expect I would be very pleased to know my brother was one of the first to travel overland on the railway I helped build. I shall write him tonight to see if he has any news.

JM

The Two Grading Crews Meet

Mr. Dan came with some news today that was rather exciting. He told me the grading crews of our Union Pacific have met up with the Chinamen working on the Central Pacific somewhere out in the deserts of Utah. The gangs worked side by side of each other and it must have been a sight. The Central Pacific got there first and picked the better terrain to work with but that didn't slow our boys down one bit. They kept working away in the opposite direction building as much grade as possible and pouring fill wherever necessary.

It seems that a bit of devilment got into our boys however. As they were making the cuts, they set off the charges of dynamite without giving those Chinamen advance notice of what they was up to. Seeing how they was so close to each other, rocks and debris rained down on the tops of those poor fellas with the Irish lads well out of sight of the hail of rocks, sending the Chinese scurrying in all directions and running for cover. The Chinamen finally had enough of that and figured turn about was fair play and set off a charge next to the Irish lads that would cause the ancient kings of Tara to sit upright in their graves. It seems the lads decided a truce was in order after that gave them proper notice when a charge was to be exploded.

Mr. Dan also said that it doesn't make any sense for the two companies to be working at cross purposes when you look at it from the government's point of view. He expects that the big men and politicians will have to sit down and decide on a meeting point. Granted, the more track we lay, the more money we make and by the same token, the less money the Central Pacific makes. Mr. Dan no doubt is much more in favor of our side making the money than the likes of those California swindlers like Crocker and Stanford. I would have to agree with Mr. Dan, especially since our crews keep earning higher wages the closer we get to the last mile of track.

The meeting also means another thing as well and that our grading crews will have to be dismissed soon. Many of them will have to go off looking for other work and soon behind them, the track laying crews will have to be dismissed as well. Those lads have not been paid in some time and I am sure any of them with a lick of sense will know the work is nearing its end and expect the Casements to be settling accounts with them. It could get real ugly if the men don't get some sort of compensation soon. The rumors will begin to flow from the mouths of gossips and the like who make trouble just for the sake of stirring the pot, just to watch their fellow workers get angered when their ain't nothing to get angry about.

I didn't mention none of this to Mr. Dan but I expect he knows already.

I don't know what I am going to do yet when we get to the end of all this but I expect I got a couple more months to figure it out. Even though I have managed to save a good bit of money, it is not enough to buy a bit of land when you consider I got nothing left over to buy the cattle, build me a house, or buy me a horse and saddle. Some drovers came through here and told me a lot of men are gathering cattle left unattended during the rebellion and taking them up north to pastures in Nebraska and even as far north as Montana.

One thing for certain, I got no use for the land around here. The drovers told me that Montana however is something that every man needs to see before the end of his life. There are still some Indians up that way but they are not nearly so murderous as the Sioux or Cheyenne and not likely to bother you unless you bother them.

I reckon I could put my money on deposit in a Denver bank and join up with an outfit to drive cattle up from Texas to Montana. At least that way I could get to see a good bit more of the country before I settle and save some more of my wages. Those drovers told me that my horse and saddle would be provided if I needed one and we get paid at the end of the drive, leaving me a large amount of wages to buy my land. That all sounds good but I told them I ain't going to ride drag no more 'cause I had enough of that during the war. They said someone with experience like me ain't likely to have to but that was up to the trail boss.

JM

I

Meeting in Promontory

I got word today that some fellow off of Jack Morrow's gang is nearby looking for me. Morrow is pretty well known out here as a low down thief and murderer whose men often dress up as Indians. They waylay travelers on their way out West, stealing their cattle and selling them supplies stolen from other trains at greatly inflated prices.

I don't know why they have business with me and I don't know if there is any truth to that rumor but I am not taking any chances. I told General Jack about it and he lent me a gun that I have tucked into my belt and hid beneath my great coat. He wished me good luck and said that if he sees Morrow and his crew first, he will let me know.

General Jack has been really good to me and a man of his outstanding character stands out in this country.

Quinn and I thought we might walk around the camp this evening to see all the people getting ready for the celebration that will come this Monday. People are pouring in from all over, many who are very important people from back East who wanted to witness the final spike being driven so they could tell their grandchildren many years from now.

There is still the usual lot that have been following the railroad crews out west such as the card sharps, gamblers and any one else that tries to make an easy living by diverting the earnings of our work gangs into their pockets with the least amount of effort.

Even still, they seem to be in high spirits as well since the event affects us all as a nation and because revelers are more willing to dig into their pockets to celebrate the event.

Around dusk as we were walking among the rows of tents, taking in all the activities and people watching, we heard the sound of a scream. Off to our side a man was dragging a woman around the corner by her wrist and it was clear by the beating she was giving the fella with her parasol she wanted no part of him. Quinn and I looked at each other and decided we must intercede since this woman appeared to be a lady, not one of the soiled doves, a camp follower or any other low woman known round here. Neither did the man appear familiar to us as well but that means nothing out in these parts since people come and go with the wind.

We ran toward the direction of where the two were putting up a ruckus and it seemed odd that no one besides ourselves should take part in this rescue of this lady. We turned the corner and who should be standing there but Foley and Cannady, with pistols drawn and leveled toward our guts. It was clear by the look on Foley's face that he was well pleased with his deception and handed the man and the woman who had so convincingly drawn us into the alley two five dollar gold pieces for their efforts. They thanked him and gave us a self congratulatory smirk, as they looked us up and down walking away to celebrate their reward for their acting skill.

"Foley?" says I. "We heard you was dead."

"Well, as you can plainly see, I am not," he replied.

I felt a sense of dread come over me that I had not felt since back at Julesburg. I knew I was either going to die or get badly hurt but I wasn't sure which. The meeting of these two startled me something awful but I started to sweat and breathe short, shallow breaths.

"What do the two of you want?" Quinn asked.

"To see you hang," retorted Foley. "Mr. Cannady of the Pinkerton's here has come a long way to find you and see that you are returned to Ireland so you can dance at the end of a rope. It seems that the Lord of the estate you worked is quite anxious to see you again. You didn't bother to say good bye when you left."

"Aye, that I didn't," agreed Quinn. "So what's this undertaker of a man paying you for your troubles?"

"We are going to split the reward put up for you," Cannady dryly noted. "A thousand pounds sterling is a lot of money, don't you think? That Lord seems very anxious to see you once again if he is willing to pay that kind of money."

"So who was that wearing your clothes was killed and mutilated by the Indians? And how did that fellow come by your clothes?" says I.

"I don't recall his name but 'tis a pity," said Foley. "He was in a hurry to get out of the territory and I was happy to oblige him. Said the law would be looking for him so seeing how he was my size and was willing to pay more than they was worth, I was glad to sell him those duds. Since I joined up with Mr. Morrow, I have made plenty of money and have a whole trunk of fine clothes.

"So, now you know how I came upon my fashions, will there be anything else you will be wanting to inquire about?" he said with a measured degree of sarcasm.

"All right then, that answers that, but what of me," I asked. "What business do we have then?"

"Oh not much," he casually replied. "I just have your ears as you took part of mine. Maybe when I am done with you, I'll let you live as a cripple assuming you survive the carving I'm going to do on ya'. That's a sight more than I did for your nigger friend and that dog of his."

So he's the one who killed Hoppin' John and Colleen! I felt a rage start swelling up in me that I could barely contain. A sweat came over me and my heart began to pound. I wasn't scared no longer.

"That dog was worth more than either of you," I hissed between clenched teeth. "And that darky more than the two of ya' put together."

I might soon get my ears cut on and I wasn't going to sit still whilst he done the cutting. I needed to think how I could get out of this mess.

"Get moving," Cannady gestured with his gun. "Put your Fenian arses into the light so I can get these shackles on you."

We turned and came out the alley the same way we came in. The sound of chains and shackles clanged together in time as we walked. Nobody bothered looking our direction, nobody we knew who might help was near by.

A makeshift wagon yard was just ahead and there were some teamsters coming in from the day's work. They were unhitching their horses and putting the harnesses in the back of the wagon since it was a little past dark. One of them had set a kerosene lamp down on the gate of his wagon so that he might better see what he was doing.

"Hold up here," said Cannady. "Move over toward that light."

Quinn and I walked that direction at a slow pace and as we were nearing the light, Quinn whispered to me under his breath, "Be ready."

"Be ready? What's that supposed to mean?" I was thinking to myself. Regardless, I watched Quinn closely out of the corner of my eye for a sign of movement so that I might run or fight or kick dirt in their eyes so we could make our escape. Whatever it was, I was not going to give up my ears for the like of a thief and murderer like Foley.

"That's far enough," said Cannady. I heard behind me the clink of the shackles landing on the ground as he threw them down behind us. "Turn around and put these on," he said.

"Here it comes," whispered Quinn. I was ready but ready for what I didn't know.

As we were turning, Quinn swept up the kerosene lamp in one fluid motion and flung it toward Foley. Surprised and blinded by the light coming at him, he held up his gun to block the oncoming lantern. The glass of the lamp shattered as it hit his revolver spraying kerosene all over him and lighting him on fire. His clothing quickly caught and the fire spread all over his body leaving him dancing around in the darkness like a human torch. He screamed in agony as he looked for a way to douse the flames but there was nothing for him to do and neither of us was going to help. He took a couple of wild shots toward us missing completely.

The look that came over Cannady's face as he saw Foley set afire was one of shock. He quickly realized he no longer held the upper hand as his own sleeve caught fire from the spray of the kerosene as it broke over Foley. He swung his arm wildly in the air trying to extinguish the flame and took no note of us while he in a panic tried to relieve himself from the searing pain that was working its way over the length of his arm.

Pulling the gun from beneath my great coat that General Jack had lent me, I lowered my pistol toward Cannady. When he saw my gun aimed at him, he looked even more terrified, the expression on his face one of panic and resignation at the same time. He quit shaking his arm for just a second as it registered that this was his last moment on earth. I pulled the trigger in a slow deliberate motion and the recoil of the weapon kicked back toward me while at the same time blowing a bright reddish orange plume toward the Pinkerton. The explosion of the powder and the slap of the projectile against his forehead left little doubt about whether I had hit my mark. This wretch of human collapsed into a heap falling face forward into the dirt.

I next swung my arm in an arc toward Foley. His whole body was ablaze at this moment and screaming at the top of his lungs about the searing pain that was working over the whole surface of his body. Thrashing about wildly, he was still holding his pistol when I pulled the trigger again. The pistol kicked back and my aim was off just a bit because he was writhing so. He staggered more slowly as the wound registered in his mind. I pulled the trigger a third time hitting him squarely in the chest and he fell over backwards.

Horses and mules were kicking and bucking around the corrals from all the excitement and braying and whinnying with all the shooting and loud noises around them. Quinn and I walked over toward Foley and began kicking dirt over his body to extinguish the flames. Soon the fire was out but his body was a heap of burned flesh that was thoroughly unpleasant to look up. Cannady's was not much better as the bullet had entered his forehead and left the back of his skull, leaving a large hole where it had exited.

My heart was still racing from the excitement but I was not shaking as I had when I fought at Julesburg. I looked around and the teamsters came over to have a look at the bodies and at us.

"You fellas all right?" one of them asked.

"Yea, I am fine. How about you Dennis?" I asked.

"Yeah," he replied with some hesitation. "But our visitors that came a calling don't seem so well off."

"Aye, that they don't," says I.

"Mister, if you want to make a few dollars for your trouble, load this trash up and haul it out to the desert and bury it," says I. "These fellows should have some money on them and whatever they have, you are welcome to as far as I care. Nobody need know about it beyond us three. Even if they did, I doubt anyone would care, knowing the likes of these two."

"Fair enough," the teamster replied. He hesitated and stared at the corpses and said, "First light tomorrow, I will haul 'em away."

After a long pause, I turned to Dennis and said to him, "So, you are a guest for a party to be held in your honor back in the old country, are you? Any thoughts of going?

"None at all," says he. "I like it in this country just fine."

"As do I," says I. "As do I."

JM

The Celebration

Today is May 10, 1869. It was a beautiful spring day here in Utah that was a bit chilly in the morning but the sun later came out to warm things to a tolerable level.

People came in from every direction. Gamblers, dignitaries, workers and reporters all converged to the point that will be remembered in history. Several photographers were walking through the crowd marking the event with flashes going off every minute.

Leading up to the ceremony, a tie made up of laurel wood was laid down with a crew of Irish bringing in one of the last pair of rails and laying it on the west side while a gang of Chinese track layers brought in the matching rail from the East. About that time, one of the men in the crowd shouted to one of the photographers on hand, "Now's the time Charley, take the shot."

Well, for the Chinese who don't speak a whole lot of English, 'shot' means a charge of dynamite is about to go off and these poor fellas dropped the rail and ran for cover expecting an explosion to come any second. The crowd cackled and hee-hawed at the sight of those Chinamen's pig-tails flying and them ducking underneath the rail cars.

It was getting on about noon and after everyone collected themselves from the show the Chinamen put on, the rail that was dropped was laid back in its place. About this time some soldiers from the cavalry who were out beating the bush looking for the Captain Charley, an Indian who was notorious for getting all liquored up and terrorizing the Mormons came up to the summit not knowing what was going on. When they were told what was happening, they were full of excitement and stood by to observe the ceremonies.

Doc Durant and Governor Stanford it was rumored were arguing who was going to strike the last blow on the spike that would secure the rails. It seemed they finally came to a meeting of the minds because the second to last was a silver spike followed by the golden one which Governor Stanford drove in. It was funny because when he took a swing at it with the sledge, he missed it clean which caused some bit of suppressed laughter among the men looking on.

Cheers, flying hats and huzzahs went up from the crowd followed by the music of the two brass bands that were in attendance after the golden spike was hammered in. The telegraph operator keyed out the message 'Done' to both Atlantic and Pacific coasts. The engine *Jupiter* from the Central Pacific and the *119* from the Union Pacific edged forward to just meet so the photographers could take a photo of the historic event. Getting some of the crowd to disperse seemed a chore for them but finally they got most of the men moved out of the way to about a hundred or so that General Dodge and Mr. Montague could be seen shaking hands in front of the two engines. One fellow from the Central Pacific standing atop the *Jupiter* passed a bottle of champagne to another atop the *119* who was holding his glass out for him. Men held their breath for the pose and the photographer declared the moment was recorded for history.

Soon the dignitaries dispersed to celebrate in their private cars while the rest of the crowd milled about after it was all done. Drinks were flowing like water that day and Mr. Dan told me later that he got plenty liquored up on Governor Stanford's champagne. The governor got up to make a speech about how the government subsidies in hindsight were a bad idea and as he sat atop of the back of General Jack, his brother's shoulders like a circus acrobat, and suggested that if he didn't like the money, he should respectfully return it to the Congress. The party seemed to enjoy the joke but it was pretty clear that the governor didn't care for it much.

I was feeling a lot of things that day. Pride about what we had done but unsure what was to come next. I turned in early that day not because I didn't want to celebrate. I just needed time to think. Not that I got much sleep with the men coming every few minutes and making enough noise to wake the dead. Things eventually died down and I dozed off to sleep at a late hour with no resolution about my thoughts or feelings about the previous days' events.

JM

It is Done

Today the work we started more than three years ago is done. The final bit of track was laid down and the two railroads met here at Promontory, Utah.

Important people from all over the country came for the celebration and I must admit I had mixed feelings about it. This wild country will never be the same after joining up these two lines and people will start pouring in here before you know it. Already soldiers made a cross country trip in less than two weeks whereas before it would be months at considerably more expense to move all their provisions.

Building this railroad is one of the greatest engineering achievements that men have ever done, right up there with the pyramids of Egypt. I have to say that being part of this is one of the proudest achievements of mine as well, even though my contribution to it was modest with just me running a crew of men laying track. Most of the men I know feel the same as well, so much more than how we felt when the war was finally over.

In hind sight, I got to see a good bit of the country on the way out here even if most of it was flat Nebraska prairie and arid Wyoming. I worked with some fine men and am sorry for losing some good ones like Hoppin' John along the way who will never know how much he meant to me and others that were counting on him. So many men got crippled or died that it would be nearly impossible to count them all and it is a down right shame about that.

What strikes me as funny now that this is all over is the railroad is a tool to help support commerce and settle the West. Although it will do those things, it also has the opposite effect also. The Sioux, Cheyenne and other Plains tribes are going to be ruined on account of this. We have pretty much killed off all of their buffalo, and the white men who pour into this part of the country are going to have no regard for their feelings about the subject. Every greenhorn and excursionist that gets off the train from the East looks at the Indian with contempt, someone to be pushed out of the way so that nothing gets in the way of working the farm the government gave them.

The Irish have something in common with them Indians. We have no land of our own as long as the English occupy it and what we have left is our language, culture and religion to give us our identity. Even at that, the English have tried to kill that off so that we would all be Englishmen but God willing, the Irish will not let them succeed. I hope for the Indians they will be able to keep what is theirs, but every Indian agent that is in charge of a reservation tries to take that away from them right off.

People will find it irresistible to wander now that the railroad is finished. Opportunity is everywhere out here for a person that is willing to work hard and I reckon that many of them Irish just getting off the boat back in Philadelphia, Boston and New York will see it that way too. The railroad will both disperse people as well as help place them. New communities spring up overnight out here in the West and I reckon that means old ones back East will have to lose people in order to create the new ones here. We got our fair share of Irish but people from all over Europe are making their way out here and some Americans too, especially those Southerners who lost their homes from carpetbaggers that bought their homes for back taxes and such. Many of the men coming out here are restless Civil War veterans who got the itch under their feet from seeing so much of the country, they feel like they got to see more.

An old way of doing things is giving way to a new one. The North and South are united on account of the war. The East and the West because of this railroad.

I still haven't found my place but I ain't done with my travels yet.

JM

Epilogue

John McGlinchey left Promontory, Utah soon after and began driving cattle herds to the Montana territory. He worked as a cowboy for nearly another decade, saving up his earnings, eventually moving to Parker County, Texas and bought a 500 acre place that he could call his own. He married a young widow named Ella Maria Brown O'Neal who had a son, William from her previous marriage and together, she and John had children of their own named John, Mary, Sallie, James, Finley, Anne, Neil and Alexander.

John McGlinchey earned his living raising cattle and driving them the short distance to the Fort Worth Stockyards where the newly constructed Southern Pacific Railway would ship them throughout the country. In addition, he also earned extra money drilling wells for other homes and farms in the area.

While John worked at manual labor his entire life, his offspring benefited from his strong work ethic. He encouraged his children to work equally hard and acquire an education. Many of his children, grandchildren and great-grand children became leaders in the community. Professions his offspring adopted include artist, judge, writer, attorneys, teacher among many others and they helped create the small community of Aledo, Texas. He and his wife modeled religious tolerance by belonging to different faiths and allowing their children to attend the church of their choice.

Dennis Quinn did indeed move to Texas and he eventually married Mary Doyle also of County Wicklow. He continued to find work with the railroads and became a teamster moving about the country as the railroad moved west. Mary eventually tired of the moves and work camps and said she would not move beyond Dallas, Texas and Dennis could stay or move with the construction crew. Dennis opted to stay and continued to earn a living as a teamster in the Dallas area.

Bibliography

Ambrose, S. (2000). *Nothing like it in the world*. New York: Simon and Schuster.

Bain, D. (1999). *Empire express*. New York: Viking.

Baker, W., & Sinclair, C. (1917). *West African folk-tales*. Berkeley: University of California Press.

Clark, D. (1973). *The Irish in Philadelphia*. Philadelphia: Temple University Press.

Dodge, G. (1910). *How we built the Union Pacific Railway*. Retrieved From Books.Google.com

Gallman, J. (2000). *Receiving Erin's children*. Chapel Hill: University of North Carolina Press.

Leavey, U., & Field, S. (1996). Irish fairy tales and legends. Dublin: O'Brien Press.

Miller, E. (2009). *A Traveler's Guide to Railroad 1869*. Mill Valley, CA: Antelope Press.

Miller, E. (2009). *Railroad 1869*. Mill Valley, CA: Antelope Press.

Mullholland, S. (1903). *The story of the 116th Regiment Pennsylvania Volunteers in the War of the Rebellion*. (L.F. Kohl, Ed.) New York: Fordham University Press.

Glossary of Terms

116th Regiment – An all Irish Army unit formed at the beginning of the Civil War comprised mainly of volunteers from the Philadelphia area.

Abolitionist – One who advocated the liberation of the slaves. In spite of the seemingly justified moral stance, abolitionists were not popular in the North and were despised in the South. Many were protestant evangelists from England who carried their message to the United States. Not surprisingly, Americans and those who suffered under British rule considered these people to be the worst sort of hypocrites.

Ancient kings of Tara – The island of Ireland, as it is known today, was composed of many kingdoms based on a loose confederation of clans. Tara was the epicenter of the most powerful kingdoms and thought by many Irish historians to be the quintessential model and the apex of Irish monarchy.

Aqueducts – a device that delivered water usually from the mountains to cities located in valleys a considerable distance away. The Romans were legendary in their construction of these public utilities and enabled construction of many of Europe's greatest cities by providing a steady, reliable source of water.

Arse – An Irish accented inflection of the word 'ass'; slang for buttocks.

Banshee – A female spirit generally recognized in Irish culture to be a warning of impending death. The scream of the banshee is noted for its eerie, shrill nature, is impossible to ignore and provides a sense of dread among those who hear it.

Blasket Islands – The westernmost islands along the Irish Coast. Western Ireland is noted for its steadfast adherence to Irish culture and language in spite of the British attempts to convert the natives to English customs and language. Because of the remote location of the Blaskets, the natives of the islands were able to resist the acculturation attempts most successfully.

Buffalo chips – Manure left by buffalo. When dried, it made an excellent fuel source for starting fires and cooking food. Many areas of the prairie were absent of trees or other alternative sources of fuel and this made a handy and readily available substitute.

Buffalo soldier – A Negro soldier. The term derived from the Native Americans observation that African Americans' hair was similar to that of a buffalo. This type of observation was not uncommon among the natives since they lived in a symbiotic state of nature and would use common frames of reference to name things.

Braves – Native American male warriors.

Camp follower – One who offered services to the railroad and their workers that were not provided by the Union Pacific. Examples include laundress, liquor peddlar, prostitute and grocer.

Casement, Dan – Brother of Jack Casement and business manager for the construction of the Union Pacific.

Casement, General Jack – a.k.a. John Stephen. Directed the construction of the Union Pacific railroad. A Civil War general for the Union forces, General Jack as he was called by his workers was noted for both his ferocious courage and his lack of stature. He never let the latter interfere with the former. Was also noted for carrying a bullwhip and running the construction crews like a military force.

Catholic Herald (newspaper) – a newspaper published in the 19th century that addressed the issues of Catholics both in the U.S. and Ireland.

Central Pacific – The California based railroad construction project that moved eastward over the Sierra Nevada Mountains to eventually meet the westbound Union Pacific in Promontory, Utah.

Cheyenne – a Native American tribe of the Great Plains.

Ciphering – A 19th century term for addition and subtraction.

Cobbler – One who makes or repairs shoes or boots.

Coffin ship – A slang term used among the Irish regarding the poorly maintained ships used to transport them from the British Isles to the United States. Owners of the ships provided minimal food and water and often times flouted the law regarding the welfare of passengers altogether. The crowded conditions, poor sanitation and lack of food and water resulted in the deaths of many passengers prior to their arrival.

Cotton to – a slang term for acceptance of a situation or proposition.

Crocker, Charles – one of the directors of the Central Pacific Railroad and placed in charge of the construction from Sacramento eastward.

Cuchullain – an Irish mythological hero noted for his bravery and military conquests.

Dandy – a 19th slang term for a middle class male that attempted to impersonate the upper class in dress, mannerisms, and hobbies. Considered by many to be an effeminate male that overdressed for occasions that called for less flamboyance.

Darkey – an alternate slang term for a Negro used widely in the 19th century.

Derringer – a small pocket sized pistol

Dodge, General Grenville – a Union Army general and railroad executive that served as the chief engineer for the construction of the Union Pacific Railroad.

Durant, Doc – a.k.a. Thomas Clark Durant. Principal stockholder of the Union Pacific Railroad and often criticized for his lack of scruples in business dealings. He created Credit Mobilier, a scheme to permit the circumvention of the rule that no one stockholder could hold more than ten percent of the Union Pacific Railroad and attempted to add multiple twists in the construction of the railroad to increase overall miles, thereby billing the U.S. government fraudulently.

Ear notching – often used as punishment by vigilante groups when the crime did not warrant the death penalty.

Eegits – slang Irish term for idiots.

Excursionist – a derogatory term for a tourist that rode westward on the rails looking for short term adventure. Many would often shoot buffalo from the window of the trains or make foolish assumptions about the west based on hearsay or conjecture.

Fenian – the name of a fraternal organization dedicated to the establishment of a free and independent Ireland.

Finn McCool – a mythical Irish hero noted for his warrior adventures.

Fishplate – a metal bar that joins two sections of rail together and is bolted in place creating in effect a single track.

Fop – a term for a man who is overly concerned with his appearance or clothes.

Gandydancer – slang for workers who laid track for the railroads. The term is thought to have derived by the synchronized goose like waddle of teams of men placing rails to be spiked into place.

Gauger – a railroad worker that determined the precise width of track by laying crosswise a measuring device from one rail to another.

Grant, Ulysses (General) – General in Chief of all Union forces during the latter part of the Civil War and Republican Party presidential candidate for 1868, subsequently elected President.

Greely, Horace – Editor of the *New York Tribune* and one of the most influential men of the latter part of the 19th century.

Hell on Wheels – a phrase coined by Editor Samuel Bowles of the Springfield, Massachusetts *Republican* to describe the makeshift collections of saloons, dance halls and brothels that located near the construction of the Union Pacific Railroad.

Hibernians – a Latin phrase used to describe the Irish, it was also a fraternal organization designed to protect the Roman Catholic Irish against attack and persecution.

House of Lords – the upper house of the English parliament, it is comparable to the U.S. Senate in the United States. The major difference is Senators are elected and Lords during the 19th century were seated because of their hereditary birth rites as members of the royal class.

Huzzah – 19th century version of hurray

Irish American (newspaper) - a newspaper published in the 19th century that addressed the issues of Catholics both in the U.S. and Ireland.

Jesus, Joseph and Mary – a phrase employed by the Irish to indicate extreme exasperation by naming all the members of the Holy Family. Irish Catholics would often call upon the saints or a specific saint to relieve them of their problems.

Little People – another term used for Leprechaun, usually male fairies that are native to Ireland and are characterized by their imaginative practical jokes played on humans.

Liverpool –England's principal seaport and trading center during the 19th century, it was the primary point of embarkation for many Irish emigrants on their way to America.

Midwife – Someone who assists in delivery of babies. Midwifery has since moved beyond this since the 19th century encompassing pre-natal care to expectant mothers through to post partum for mother and child.

Minie-ball – a high caliber rifled projectile widely used during the Civil War resulting in enormous casualties. Wounded soldiers often faced amputations or dismemberment from wounds and striking a vital organ nearly always resulted in death.

Mormons – a term used to apply to members of the Church of Jesus Christ of Latter Day Saints. Mormon was another term used disparagingly in the 19th century to denote one who practiced polygamy.

Morrow, Jack – The leader of a gang of thugs noted for dressing as Indians and robbing west bound migrants. He would then re-sell supplies he stole from previous robberies at greatly inflated prices. Morrow also contracted as a supplier to the Union Pacific Railroad.

Moyamensing – A working class neighborhood in South Philadelphia occupied primarily by Irish immigrants during the 19th century.

Mutilation – A tactic employed by Native American tribes to prevent the victim of a battle from retaliating in the afterlife. Many tribes believed that by mutilating a victim, it will not allow him to take revenge on the victor, nor would it allow him to craft weapons or hunt for food. Settlers to the Plains often attributed the practice of mutilation to savagery when in reality it was self preservation in the mind of the Native American.

O'Connell, Daniel – An Irish patriot that advocated Catholic Emancipation and dissolution of the union between Ireland and England. He was jailed by the British for sedition.

Paddy – A derogatory slang term used to describe the Irish.

Pawnee – A Plains Indian tribe who made their homes along the Platte River in Nebraska.

Pinkerton – A generic term for a member of the Pinkerton National Detective Agency. Members in the late 19th century were often hired out as private security or bounty hunters. Their methods were criticized for their unscrupulousness and after a period of time, were not allowed to work for some state and federal government agencies.

Paymaster – one who dispersed the wages and paid accounts owed.

Pony Express – a short lived mail delivery service that went from St. Joseph, Missouri to Sacramento, California. Horses and riders rode specific lengths carrying satchels of mail and then transferred them to other riders who would continue to the next junction where another rider would take the hand off of mail, much like a relay in modern day track meet.

Quartermaster – a soldier that distributes provisions for the Supply Corps for the Army.

Radicals – An extreme wing of the Republican Party. Members were not satisfied with lenient unification terms proposed by Lincoln or other moderates with the former Confederate States but wanted them exceedingly punished resulting in a geographic and ideological schism between North and South that exists today.

Reconstruction – The period after the Civil War in which those states belonging to the Confederacy were restructured politically and legally to meet criteria for reunification established by a Northern Republican dominated Congress. The term in the South was often employed as a synonym for harsh measures imposed unwillingly against Southerners by the victors of the conflict which resulted in enormous loss of power and property. Military and political policies during the Reconstruction period often times created a wider gulf between North and South rather than help unify the government.

Red Cloud – a great chief of the Oglala branch of the Sioux tribe

Riding Drag – the least preferred place when driving cattle, this position was held at the rear of the herd. Novices were usually assigned this spot because they were the most junior members of the outfit. Those riding drag could count on swallowing plenty of dust since the cloud of dirt lifted from the cattle usually moved back toward the 'drag' spot.

Rosary – a set of beads used by members of the Catholic Church in a systemic prayer ritual.

Shantytown – another name for Hell on Wheels.

Sherman's March through Georgia – marked a turning point in warfare, Sherman demonstrated that he and his troops could march anywhere throughout the South, thereby destroying morale among citizens of the Confederacy. The march was noted for its ruthlessness as well bringing a secondary concept, total warfare, to the forefront. The idea of total warfare is armies are merely extensions of the political machinery. The people create the political machinery and consequently, the Army. In Sherman's view, it was necessary to destroy one to destroy the other.

Sierra Nevada – a high range of mountains that border California and Nevada.

Sioux or Lakota – are a tribe of Native Americans whose traditional territory encompassed the northern Plains area of the United States and parts of Lower Canada.

Spiker – one who drove the spikes into the ties and rail tracks.

Squaw – a term used in a derogatory manner to describe a female Native American.

Soiled Dove – a synonymous term for prostitute

Stanford, Leland – President of the Central Pacific Railroad during the construction of the Intercontinental Railroad.

Stanley, Henry Morton – perhaps the most famous journalist of the late 19th century, rivaled only by Samuel Clemens (Mark Twain) in overall readership about his journeys.

Stoics – a member of a Greek sect of philosophers that de-emphasized human emotion as a driving force, considering it a destructive element of the human condition.

Tender – a railway worker that place the rails over the ties and sub-foundation with the use of tongs.

Ulster – is a province in Northern Ireland, widely settled by the Scotch Protestants after the victory of William of Orange over James II. Irish Catholics native to the region were excluded from political process based on their religion however both Scots and Irish were discriminated against by the ruling English. This resulted in a religious and cultural schism among the Irish which exists to this day.

Usury – charging exorbitant and unfair interest for a loan.

Vicksburg campaign – a siege led against the city of Vicksburg, Mississippi by General Ulysses Grant. Capturing Vicksburg essentially assured control of the Mississippi River for the Union forces and the surrender of the city occurred on July 4, 1863. The date was chosen purposely since the commanding general of the Confederate forces assumed rightly so that greater terms could be negotiated if surrender occurred on this day. The city of Vicksburg and many former Confederates that fought in the conflict did not celebrate the Fourth of July for many decades to come.

Walking Boss – a foreman placed in charge of a small group of railroad workers

Young, Brigham – political and spiritual leader of the Church of Jesus Christ of Latter-day Saints who were better known as Mormons during the latter part of the 19th century. He negotiated a contract to build part of the rail line for the Union Pacific Railroad in the Utah territory. He and his followers were never paid but eventually came to a settlement regarding the money owed them by the Union Pacific.

Notes

Made in the USA
Charleston, SC
23 June 2010